We'll Laugh Again

Also by Art Buchwald

We'll Laugh Again

Art Buchwald

G. P. Putnam's Sons

New York

2002

G. P. Putnam's Sons
Publishers Since 1838
a member of
Penguin Putnam Inc.
375 Hudson Street
New York, NY 10014

Library of Congress Cataloging-in-Publication Data

Buchwald, Art.
We'll laugh again / by Art Buchwald.
p.   cm.
ISBN 0-399-14892-2
1. United States—Politics and government—
1993–2001—Humor.   2. United States—Social life and
customs—1971—Humor.   I. Title.
PS3503.U1828W45   2002   2001057870
814'.54—dc21

Printed in the United States of America
1   3   5   7   9   10   8   6   4   2

This book is printed on acid-free paper. ♾

Book design by Stephanie Huntwork

Acknowledgments

Cathy Clark helped select and edit the columns for this book, and she compiled the manuscript. Hillery Borton and Phyllis Grann completed the editing. I did the FedExing.

ART BUCHWALD

Contents

Part Three

Part Four

Part Five

Part Six

Introduction

Most of this book was edited before September 11, 2001. At the time, it dealt with the last eleven years in Washington, which turned out to be the most glorious time of our lives. Everything from a president's peccadilloes to the silliness of the decade was included. The original title was *Those Were the Days,* with a subtitle, *We Thought They Would Never End.* After September 11, I changed the title because some readers might have misinterpreted it, and I have included the columns written after that date.

The title I selected is *We'll Laugh Again.* It is based on a story I heard when President John F. Kennedy was shot. Mary McGrory, the columnist, said to Pat Moynihan, "We'll never laugh again."

And Moynihan replied, "Mary, we'll laugh again, but we'll never be young again."

I loved Bill Clinton because he made me a very rich man. When he said he never lied to us, I built a swimming pool in the back of my house. When he said he had an affair with Monica Lewinsky, I bought a new Lexus. When he pardoned Marc Rich, I bought a house on Martha's Vineyard.

I was disappointed when the publisher didn't offer me ten million dollars to write my version of these events.

Another subject of the last eleven years that contributed to my large fortune was the high cost of drugs, which reached a point where, instead of swallowing them, people started putting them in their safe-deposit boxes as investments. For example, a Valium pill in its original cotton was sold at Sotheby's for $45,000. A blood pressure pill from the Annenberg collection went for $60,000, and a Prozac pill from Ted Turner's Blue Period went for $76,000.

I was lucky to find out from sources that I cannot reveal the names of heavy hitters who slept in the Lincoln Bedroom in the White House, and how much they paid to sleep there.

I was the first to uncover the existence of a government program to retrain unemployed autoworkers as heart surgeons.

Without fear this book reveals how the telephone company is ruining your life and how much it will cost you.

I have dealt with hard money versus soft money. Politicians will do anything to get their hands on soft money because it is so much more sexy to touch.

I discovered that people forced out of their buildings to take a smoke are ministered to by a priest.

In this book you will learn why the Supreme Court ruled that it is legal to medicate the insane in order to execute them.

In these pages I announce the greatest invention of the twentieth century—Viagra.

All these articles are top secret and have been verified by an unidentified source who did not answer my telephone calls.

AFTER SEPTEMBER 11, 2001

We Won't Be Young Again

WHEN PRESIDENT KENNEDY WAS KILLED, my friend Mary McGrory said to Senator Pat Moynihan, "We'll never laugh again."

And Senator Moynihan replied, "Mary, we'll laugh again, but we'll never be young again."

That is the way I felt last Tuesday.

The first feeling was disbelief. These things only happen in bad Hollywood movies.

I saw on the screen rubble and flames and smoke and death—and while I wanted to turn the TV off, I couldn't. I stared and didn't know what I was staring at. I said, "We'll laugh again, but we'll never be young again."

As the day wore on, I felt what so many people were feeling—anger. I wanted to strike out, but I didn't know whom to strike out against. Terrorist names were bandied about, and I wanted to kill all of them. It was a futile thought because many of them were killing themselves. "We'll laugh again, but we'll never be young again."

Then I started to think about how they managed to damage the most powerful country in the world. How could they have hijacked four airliners at the same time and hit three of their targets? Where were the sophisticated pilots trained? How many countries harbored them while they prepared for their mission? "We'll laugh again, but we'll never be young again."

My next emotion was anger at the CIA and all the intelligence organizations that failed to discover the plots of the terrorists who planned them. It's not a rational thought, but at this moment none of my thoughts are rational.

Then another thought ran through my head: Why do you need a $100-billion missile shield when our own hijacked planes can do the destruction? The United States is prepared to go to war, but whom do we declare war on? When it comes to the defense of our country, all bets are now off.

I watch the same pictures over and over again. The buildings on fire, and tumbling down, the soot on the faces of the rescued and the rescuers, and I know I'm entering a new world and things will never be the same.

How much freedom will I have to give up for safety? Nobody knows.

The only thing I can be sure of—"We'll laugh again, but we'll never be young again."

Another Day of Infamy

IT'S HARD TO ADMIT THIS, but I was in World War II. The Japanese had made their attack on Pearl Harbor, and the country was prepared to fight back.

Those of us who are still alive remember Roosevelt's declaration of war. The country's youth were prepared to go, and the country's civilians were prepared to support them.

I thought of this when the president and the country's leaders said, "Whatever we call it, we are at war."

My mind went back to December 7, 1941, when a group of us sixteen- and seventeen-year-olds were in a bowling alley in Forest Hills, New York.

When the news came over the radio, we assured one another that we would be able to vanquish the Japanese (let's be frank, we called them "Japs" at that time) in weeks. We cited the shoddy goods they sold to the world and their lack of oil.

Swept up in the country's patriotism and inspired by John Wayne, I joined the Marines.

I'm not telling this story for any reason except that this war is going to be different from all other wars.

The president vowed we would not only hunt down the terrorists but also the countries that give them safe harbor. No one argues with this, but the problem is unlike the one we faced against the Japanese and Germans. This time we are up against an unknown enemy.

The name Osama bin Laden keeps coming up. At least his is the face of an enemy and, therefore, if we prove he did it we will have someone we can focus on and kill with impunity. If he was in concert with other terrorist groups spread out across the Middle East (Afghanistan, Pakistan, Iran, Iraq, Libya, Algeria, Sudan), the targets will be much tougher.

The name of the game now is global warfare, and young men will once again line up to go—but go where?

The simplest way is to fight our enemy from the air. But you have to kill an awful lot of people, and the terrorists could still get away.

There was no confusion amongst the Allies in World War II. We knew who the enemy was and they knew who we were. It even took an atomic bomb to make them listen to reason.

I know the guys at the bowling alley in Forest Hills would have a solution. I wish they were with me now.

Scoundrels in Our Closet

NOT ONLY HAVE THE PATRIOTS banded together for their country, but the scoundrels are also hard at work trying to figure out how to make a buck out of what we call a war.

These are just a few of the scams that people are coming up with:

- telemarketing schemes where boilerplate callers are telephoning senior citizens asking them to contribute to charities that don't exist

- gas stations doubling the price of their products for no reason
- dishonest real estate agents willing to gouge companies and people who have lost office space in downtown New York

If it's a long war, as Washington predicts, we will certainly have a black market where the scoundrels will profit on any product that is in short supply.

This country has not had a black market since World War II. I wouldn't call Nate, who had the grocery store around the corner, a serious black marketer, but he did put fear into my father.

Every time Pop walked into the store, Nate would say, "I can only give you two jars of peanut butter."

My father didn't know that peanut butter was not rationed and you could buy as much as you wanted.

When Pop heard he was limited to only two jars he protested. "Nate, I'm a regular customer. My son is in the service. Can't I have three jars?"

Nate said no.

All during the war Pop visited the store and demanded his two-jar ration. He did this because Nathan was his friend.

I know this because when I came home on leave in 1945, I opened the clothes closet and found it stuffed with what must have been a thousand jars of peanut butter.

"What are we doing with all this peanut butter?" I asked.

Pop replied, "Nate said that there was going to be a shortage, so he sold me two jars every week."

I said, "The war is over, and we'll never be able to eat all of this. Take it back."

Pop said, "Nate won't take it back. He says he is in peanut butter up to his ears."

Although the world won't be the same, some things will never change. I thought of this Saturday while watching the Miss America show on television.

The organizers said they would go ahead with the program because they wanted to show the terrorists that Miss America is not going to be pushed around.

The world will never change as long as thousands of press agents attempt to get their clients' names in the newspaper.

They are not scoundrels; they are just doing their jobs.

So while most people will be changed, there are a few who will always be the same. That's the way the world crumbles.

This Way of Life

FROM NOW ON the question will be how much security vs. how much freedom this country will need to survive.

I had this conversation with Miguel Santa Cruz, a friend from a South American country. I told him, "I want fail-safe security, but I also want to say anything I want to. That is what this war is all about. For example, if we're going to keep our freedoms, that means defending Jerry Falwell and Pat Robertson even if I don't agree with anything they say."

Miguel said, "Who are Jerry Falwell and Pat Robertson?"

"They are TV preachers. So if we're really going to preserve our way of life I have to support Jerry Falwell. Just after the terrorist attacks he told Pat Robertson on television that God was angry with us because this country supports homosexuality, abortion rights, atheism, the American Civil Liberties Union and the People for the American Way. It was not the message Americans wanted to hear at that moment, and the next day he retracted it."

"What's wrong with that?"

I said, "He had a right to say it. The entire fabric of this country is woven around the First Amendment. We are permitted to say anything we want to. I have my own feelings about God, and they are not anything like Falwell's and Pat Robertson's. I'm for planned parenthood. I give money to the American Civil Liberties Union, and I'm against prayers in school. Therefore, I have to let the TV preachers have their mikes to protect my own way of life."

"What about atheists?" Miguel asked me. "Do you support the godless people?"

"In America you can find any cause you want to. When it comes to publications, you can buy papers on the extreme right or the extreme left, and I can't stomach either one of them. But if they aren't permitted to publish what they want to, then neither can the *Washington Post* and the *New York Times*."

"What about demonstrations?"

"You are protected by the Constitution, even though most Americans don't protest in the streets. The thing that scares me is that people will do anything in the name of security, while they are really talking about taking our freedoms away. They are saying free speech will give aid and comfort to the enemy, but if we can't say what we want to, we'll give terrorists more aid and comfort than ever before."

"So that means if your way of life survives you have to let everyone say anything they want to?"

"You don't have to agree with everybody, but you can't stop anyone from saying out loud what he is thinking. It's what we are all about."

Miguel said, "I have a cousin who is always yelling about the environment, and he keeps throwing his body against a nuclear plant."

I said, "He's lucky to live here."

What's Funny

ONE OF THE THINGS I keep hearing is if we are going to weather this crisis we have to retrieve our senses of humor. It is easier said than done. There are two people involved in humor: the purveyor of humor and the receiver of it. If the purveyor does not get the receiver to laugh, then he has failed to deliver. You have to be on the same laugh track as your audience to be considered funny.

I thought of this after the attacks on America. Everyone kept telling me that I had to make people laugh. But at what?

I told Bob Koehler, my editor, "I have permission to make people laugh, but I have no idea what they will laugh at."

"You are suffering from an irony crisis," he said.

I replied, "Well, I can't make fun of Washington."

"I should hope not."

"And the president is no longer funny. In the past when I mentioned Bush, people laughed—uproariously. Now when you talk about him you have to treat him like another Abraham Lincoln. It's no time to make fun of Congress—or for that matter anybody in government. I'm facing a vast wasteland."

"I hope you don't mention anything about flying," Bob said.

"Do you think I'm crazy?"

Then he said, "What about Osama bin Laden's beard?"

"His beard is funny to some people, but not to others. Afghanistan is not funny. Pakistan is, though nobody knows where it is.

"There is absolutely nothing remotely funny about the stock market. If you even mention the economy, people will throw rocks at you."

Bob said, "I wouldn't blame them. What about mothers? They used to be funny."

"Not anymore. I scratched them from my repertoire. You can't make people laugh when they have no center. The audience has to know what to laugh at, and they are not ready for that yet. Jay Leno and David Letterman are trying to make people laugh, but they don't have their hearts in it."

Bob said, "The only way we're going to beat the terrorists is to go back to normal times. But when it comes to humor, what is a normal time? To quote Richard Leiby of the *Washington Post,* 'Nobody wants a wiseacre at a funeral.'"

Then Bob said, "All the stand-up comics are falling down."

"Why is that?"

"Because they are filled with fear. If they tell jokes about their girlfriends and no one laughs, they will be out in the street."

I said, "I guess irony will come back, but I'm not sure I can wait."

Big Spenders Wanted

PRESIDENT BUSH IS SENDING OUT several messages. One is that we have to spend money to defeat the terrorists, whose main purpose is to destroy our economy. In order to do this he said we should take vacations, buy things and fly on the airlines.

In past wars we were always asked to tighten our belts. This time we are told to spend, spend, spend.

If we don't, we may reach the point where the FBI starts doing spot checks on who is spending and who isn't.

Two agents go to the home of Martin Blitz. One says, "Blitz, our records say you haven't spent any money this week. How do you think that's going to look in Afghanistan?"

"I was going to buy a new car as soon as the crisis was over."

"You are part of the crisis. If you don't buy a car now, then the American flag means nothing to you."

"I don't have enough money to buy a car," Blitz says.

"Then go out and borrow some. Use everything on your credit card. This is no time to save. Look, fellow, every day you don't spend money, Osama bin Laden will laugh at you. He knows what the gross national product is. What about buying new golf clubs?"

Blitz says, "I don't play golf."

"How about a ski trip?"

Blitz says, "I don't ski."

"It's as good a time as any to learn."

"I thought in wartime you were supposed to tighten your belt and even save the silver from your cigarette packages."

"This is a different kind of war. Now when are you going to take your next flight?"

"I'm afraid to fly."

"Man, you've got to fly to prove we're the greatest country in the world. This is what we want you to do. We want you to book a flight and take your family to Disneyland. Then take a cruise to the Caribbean. If you do this, we'll remove you from our list of suspected tightwads."

Blitz says, "I'll do it. This country needs me now more than ever. God bless our department stores."

This is only one scenario of what could happen. I don't think that our leaders are going to call in the FBI at this time, but they may have started profiling people who refuse to spread the wealth.

I looked out the window yesterday, and Blitz was out there discussing plans for a swimming pool.

He was a man after George W. Bush's own heart.

It's Only a Film

SOME YEARS BACK I WROTE a piece about taking my son to a movie about World War II. I explained that in the movie the Germans were the bad guys, but now they are good guys. The Russians were good guys during the war, but because they wanted to kick the Germans out of Berlin after the war, they became the bad guys.

I thought about this recently when I took my ten-year-old grandson to the movies. It was one of those bloody, shoot-'em-up films with all the bad guys blasting the good guys and then, at the end, the good guys wasting the bad guys. When we walked out I asked him, "How could you stand all that violence?"

He replied, "Grandpa, it's only a movie."

I turned on the television a few weeks later and said, "This is not a movie you're watching but the real thing."

He looked at the screen and said, "Where are the bad guys?"

"They are all dead. They all committed suicide, but they took so many good guys with them. They were terrorists."

He kept looking at the screen.

Then he said, "In the movies the good guys always kill the bad guys at the end."

"The reason Hollywood made so many violent films is because the young people who wanted them knew they were only movies. Americans got their kicks from violence on the screen and on TV. The kids loved it. We never thought we would see the real thing on the evening news."

"Are all the bad guys dead?"

"The ones who did it are dead. But we have to find the bad guys who planned all of it and are still alive. Maybe someday we will kill them."

"I'll bet James Bond could find them."

I said, "James Bond would have a tough time doing it even with all his lethal toys."

"I've seen Arnold Schwarzenegger throw a hundred guys off a cliff."

"Yes, he did that, but Arnold would have as much trouble throwing these bad guys off the cliffs as the CIA."

"What about Bruce Willis?"

"He can't do it either. No one in Hollywood can do it."

He said, "Does this mean that they are not going to make any movies where lots of people get killed?"

"Not for a while. What you are seeing now is too much for any of us to absorb."

"Where are the bad guys now?"

"They are everywhere and nowhere. No one knows how to play this one, and never will. What you are watching is not a film but history."

My grandson became very quiet.

He said, "It won't be like it used to be, Grandpa."

I told him, "It will be different and so will we."

Football Is Not the Same

I WAS WATCHING THE REDSKINS game last Sunday on TV, and it was different from any pro football game I had ever watched before. Then it dawned on me that for the first time I didn't care who won.

I was watching it with Bill Schlossenberg. In the past, when the Redskins let the Giants intercept a pass, Schlossenberg and I would be screaming at the set and jumping up and down in frustration. This time we just sat there, without saying a word.

Finally I said, "I feel guilty about even watching the game. At this very moment we're dropping bombs on Kabul, and you and I are looking at a stupid football game."

Schlossenberg said, "But our government says in order to fight terrorism we have to go back to living the way we used to. Football is something they can never take away from us."

"Right now," I told him, "while we are watching the Redskins get penalized for roughing the passer, Donald Rumsfeld is on the other channel telling the nation why we have to fire cruise missiles and bombs on Afghanistan and also feed the Afghan people."

Schlossenberg asked, "Should we listen to what Rumsfeld has to say instead of watching stupid football?"

"Wouldn't Osama bin Laden love that. Football is what America is all about. If we turn it off, then what are our boys fighting for?"

"Does Rumsfeld think we can do both—throw bombs in war and throw bombs in football?"

"Yes."

The Redskins threw another interception.

"Who cares? It's only a game," Schlossenberg said.

I said, "Remember the days when football was everything? We used to talk about it all week long. We wouldn't go out of the house if the game was on, and we wouldn't make any social appointments if the game was on TV Monday night."

Schlossenberg said, "And if we were lucky and got to go to a game, we wore Redskin beanies and carried Redskin flags in our hands. We had team spirit and yelled until we got hoarse. And we were grown-ups, not kids. Do you think we'll ever have that spirit again?"

"I don't think it will ever be the same. Our priorities are different. Why should we care if the Giants beat the Redskins?"

"Then why are we watching?"

"Probably just out of habit. For a long time it was one of the things we cared about."

"Do the Redskins care that we don't care?"

"I'm not sure, and frankly, I don't give a damn."

"Let's switch to CNN and find out how the Air Force is doing against the Taliban. That's the real game now."

Herb

I TAKE TIME OUT from what is going on right now to say goodbye to the cartoonist Herb Block. The words "great American" have been used too frequently in our lives, but my "greatest American" was Herb. He satirized and ridiculed the hypocrisy of his country for fifty-three years. He took on everyone, including presidents, world leaders and all the power brokers in the United States. We needed him very badly to protect us from the scoundrels.

Presidents had a hard time when they were depicted by Herb. He was responsible for more canceled *Washington Post* subscriptions than anyone else on the paper.

Herb and I were friends. He kidded me that I had an easy job during the Nixon years, and I replied, "Not as easy as yours."

The papers were full of print and the president could miss an article that was critical of him, but all it took was five seconds to scan a Herblock cartoon to have the person ridiculed go up the wall.

Although the *Washington Post* was constantly being canceled by the White House, people say Nixon still looked at the editorial page when no one was watching.

I give Herb full credit for Nixon resigning. Nixon couldn't survive the drawings of him unshaven and coming out of the sewer.

When Nixon said, "I am not a crook," Herb bragged that he finished his drawing in fifteen minutes.

Other presidents did not escape Herblock's pen if he thought they were up to no good.

Eisenhower, John F. Kennedy, Lyndon Johnson and every president up to George Bush the second felt the Herblock needle.

One of his favorite targets was Senator Joe McCarthy, who waged a war against innocent people by claiming they were communists. While the country was confused, Herb gave us a McCarthy with a four-day-old beard so we would be sure to know he was the bad guy.

While Herb sketched with his poison pen, in everyday life he was a very gentle man, trusted by people in all walks of life.

One of the things that bugged him was when someone tried to give him an idea for a cartoon. He always said he got very uptight because if someone else mentioned it to him he felt he couldn't use it. I think our friendship was based on the fact that I never said, "Hey Herb, have I got a good idea for you."

Herb never gave away the original cartoon, but he xeroxed copies for the people who requested them. He got upset when someone he satirized asked for a signed copy of the drawing. If a person he had just done a number on wanted the cartoon, he considered it a bad day.

Herb Block was a very young ninety-one years old. He was drawing more brilliantly at the end than ever before. We grieve his passing—at the same time we're grateful he was with us for such a long time.

Mixed Signals

MORE THAN EVER BEFORE, Americans are living on sound bites. Unfortunately the bites are sending out different messages.

The other day I saw a high government official spokesman say, "Be calm and alert at the same time. Go about your business as you always do, but if you see anything suspicious call the FBI."

On the next channel an anthrax expert said, "At it's worst, if delivered by terrorists, it could kill thousands of people."

I hit the TV clicker and the announcer said, "Only a few people in Florida and New York were exposed, so there is no reason for panic."

Attorney General John Ashcroft said, "We have our people on the scene right now. To show you can't be intimidated by the enemy, go to a football game or a movie or just have a barbecue in the backyard."

"It is time to move on," the Pentagon spokesman said. "The Air Force and Navy are pounding Afghanistan day and night hitting only military targets."

The next channel showed the president in the Oval Office. He warned Americans not to have the jitters. "Don't get carried away. Americans should not use this opportunity to pick on somebody who doesn't look like you or doesn't share your religion."

He was upbeat, so I went to another channel where the announcer said that the FBI has warned that there will possibly be more assaults on America. The bureau said people should be calm but at the same time highly alert. The FBI said they did not know where the attack would be coming from and would not reveal where they got their information.

I alternated between cool and panic. I wanted to believe I was safe from anthrax; at the same time I felt like I wanted to move to Canada.

My surfing continued. One station was telling me all our allies were steadfast and united. The next station said we could never keep our friends in the Moslem world if we bombed Iraq.

What confused me was that the experts each had a different opinion. One station had Henry Kissinger saying one thing, and Ariel Sharon saying the opposite.

I got a glass of water and then went back to the set. The good news from intelligence sources said bin Laden was either hiding out in Kabul, holed up in a cave in the mountains, or had fled to Uzbekistan. It was good news.

But the evening news reported the food drops in Afghanistan were a bust and not getting to the people who need it. This was bad news.

I was about to throw in the towel when I finally hit a program that didn't make me panic or need to be vigilant. It was *Who Wants to Be a Millionaire?* For the first time I had a good night's sleep.

Watch Thy Neighbor

I'LL GO ALONG WITH ANYTHING the attorney general asks of me, but I worry about where we draw the line reporting anyone who looks suspicious.

He said we should go about our business but be vigilant at all times. As soon as Attorney General Ashcroft made his plea, everyone in the neighborhood became paranoid.

A week later I looked out the window and saw Mrs. Tumulty, from across the street, going through my garbage.

I ran out and said, "What the heck are you doing?"

She said, "You throw away more beer bottles than you have to. I'm going to call the FBI."

"We had a dinner party—sue me."

Later on that day I noticed that Wellspring, who lives down the street, was walking a new dog. "What's up?" I asked him.

He replied, "I traded in my French poodle for a police dog. Do you mind if he sniffs under your car?"

"Be my guest," I said.

The dog sniffed, and much to my relief he found nothing.

I asked, "Have you had any success so far?"

He said, "I thought I had gotten lucky when I found white powder in Stevens's tennis shoes, but it turned out to be Johnson's Baby Powder. The Centers for Disease Control said I did the right thing to check it out."

That afternoon I went to the shopping mall and ran into Harvey DeLouise. He was carrying a bag from Macy's. "What have you got in the bag, Harvey?"

"A sleeping bag. What have you got in your bag?"

I replied, "A CD player."

Harvey said, "Do you mind if I look?"

"Only if I can look in your bag."

We searched each other's shopping bags and found nothing suspicious. I said, "You can't be too careful."

Harvey said, "If I ever make big money, I'm going to hire a bodyguard."

Later I bought an ice cream cone from Ben & Jerry's. The man behind the counter said to me, "Have a nice day."

My antennae went up. What did he mean by that? I didn't know him, so why would he want me to have a nice day? Maybe it was a code. I made a mental note that the ice-cream scooper should be watched.

I must admit, it's harder to go about my business than the attorney general says. Once you become suspicious of everyone, you can't stop.

Just yesterday I bought a super hi-fi microphone that can pick up what my neighbors are saying in their bedrooms.

Stick 'Em Up

THE ORDERS FROM ON HIGH say we must be calm and go about our business just as we did before. I'm not sure this goes for everybody.

The other day a man in a ski mask walked into the Marigold Savings Bank.

He slid a note to the teller that read, "Give me whatever you have in your drawer."

"What on earth are you doing?"

"I'm robbing your bank."

"What for?"

"We've been told to do our normal things. Sticking up banks is what I do for a living. America is not going to let the terrorists scare us bank robbers into stopping doing what we do best."

"Do you mind taking off your mask so that our cameras can get good pictures of you?"

"I always wear a ski mask when I pull a heist. Now hurry up. I have a plane to catch, and I'm afraid to fly."

"Do you have photo identification?"

"I do, but what good does it do if I'm wearing a ski mask?"

"You are probably right. Now the suitcase you handed me to put the money in. Did you pack it yourself?"

"Please, just empty out the drawer and let me get on with my job."

"Did anyone else touch this bag before you handed it to me through the window?"

"What do you think I am, a double-crossing Taliban terrorist? I'm for America."

The teller said, "You don't have to get cheeky about it. Osama bin Laden has robbed many banks during his reign. If you are a terrorist, the money you rob from us will be frozen by the Treasury Department and you will not be able to spend it."

The robber said, "I've never dealt with somebody like this. Don't you ever panic when you're held up?"

"I would, but I've been told if I lose my cool I'll be fired. Do you have a permit for that gun?"

"No. You want to make something of it? Give me twenties, fifties and hundred-dollar bills. And also throw in a hundred Cipro pills."

"We don't have any Cipro in the bank."

"Why not?"

"It could cause panic."

"All right, how about a gas mask?"

The teller replied, "You have to have a minimum of five hundred dollars in your checking account before we can issue you a gas mask. Okay, the bag is full. I hope you have a nice day."

At this moment the FBI moved in and nabbed the bank robber. As he was dragged out he yelled, "Why don't the government people let us live the normal lives we had before!"

The Home Front Answer Man

THE HOME FRONT ANSWER MAN will answer your questions. These are the ones most frequently asked:

Question: Do I need a gas mask?

Answer Man: Everyone needs a gas mask—it is not to protect you from anthrax, but to protect you from secondhand smoke.

Q: I found a gas mask in the attic that came from World War II. How much is it worth?

A: The last one that sold on the *Antiques Road Show* went for $4,000. But it was made in Germany.

Q: I am going to a black-tie dinner party. Should I take my gas mask with me?

A: Yes. But remove it when eating corn on the cob. Then put your mask on again when you ask someone to dance.

Q: I have had trouble using a cell phone when wearing a gas mask. What should I do?

A: Get a smaller cell phone.

Q: When buying a gas mask, is the color of it an important factor?

A: Yes, it is. For example, you should never wear a chartreuse shirt with a brown mask or a black mask with an orange suit. If you're going to buy one off the rack, make sure it fits over the eyes. Gas masks should always be dry-cleaned.

Q: Speaking of biological warfare, will Viagra do the same for you as Cipro?

A: The tests are not all in yet. Bob Dole says Viagra should only be taken in place of Cipro when you are fearful and suffering from erectile dysfunction.

Q: I panic easily. What should I do?

A: Eat chicken soup and drink lots of fluids.

Q: We sold weapons to our enemies who used to be our friends, and we are selling weapons to our friends who were formerly our enemies. How's business?

A: Very good. An example is Russia, who in the past was our enemy but is now our friend. Another is the Taliban, who were our friends but are now our enemies. The reason we keep selling everyone weapons is because it is then cheaper to manufacture arms for our own defense.

Q: I notice that 50 percent of the experts on television news shows have beards and 50 percent don't. Who knows more?

A: Bearded experts look like they know more because when they answer a question they keep tugging on their beards. Clean-shaven experts, including women, know as much as the bearded ones, but they don't make a big deal out of it.

Q: My wife and I are divorced. Do I have to pay alimony while the war is on?

A: Yes, because it will show the terrorists we are not afraid of them.

Q: The president said he wants Osama bin Laden "dead or alive." Which side am I on?

A: That's the stupidest question I have ever heard.

Time for Good News

THERE IS SO MUCH BAD NEWS going around that it's time to take a rest and give you some good news.

The first good news is that Michael Jordan has come out of retirement and is playing heads-up basketball for the Washington Wizards. His salary and endorsements alone could jump-start the economy.

Barry Bonds of the San Francisco Giants broke Mark McGwire's home-run record. This means the stock market has hit bottom and will soon recover again.

When Cal Ripkin of the Baltimore Orioles played his final game, economists told the individual investor to start buying again.

The good news from Niger, Africa, is the discovery of a 110-million-year-old giant crocodile. It is forty feet long, has a six-foot-long jaw, and it roamed Central Africa eating dinosaurs for lunch. Scientists are still studying how this fits into the economy.

When Jennifer Lopez married Chris Judd, they had a lavish wedding on a mountaintop. There were 750 guests and 10,000 white and pastel rosebuds flown in for the occasion. The wedding proves what Alan Greenspan has been saying—that people are in a spending mood. He said the lavishness of the wedding is a sign that brides can now go ahead and plan bigger and more spectacular weddings. This is the first indication that Greenspan's interest-rate-cutting policies are starting to work.

Due to uncertainties in the world, the game Monopoly is coming back. Experts say if every person in the United States bought Park Place and Boardwalk we would climb out of the recession in weeks.

I saw a man on TV who won $9 million in the lottery. He said, "The best way to help the economy is to buy a winning lottery ticket. The reason the country is in a recession is Americans are not gambling enough. Now that I won I am going to spend it like there is no tomorrow, and other people should follow my example."

Good news from Great Britain. Prince William, now a freshman at Scotland's St. Andrews University, has discovered girls and, more important, they have discovered him. This is a big boost for the Eurodollar.

O. J. Simpson beat a road rage charge in Florida. This proves that road rage pays.

NASA finally got a spacecraft up to Mars, where it will send back pictures that may or may not tell us whether there was life on the planet. Investment bankers are willing to invest in the Red Planet once the pictures come back.

Oprah Winfrey was on *People*'s list of best-dressed women. Among *People*'s worst-dressed women of 2001 was Meg Ryan, who *People* said looked like a rock star in *Mary Poppins*.

While this is good news, the dress designers are unanimous in bringing out bright colors and chic pantsuits with a military motif to show where American women stand.

If Seventh Avenue believes this is the way to fight terrorism, can the bond market be far behind?

A Real Celebrity

MORE AND MORE PEOPLE are having their fifteen minutes of fame. The other day, I saw a man on the street who looked very familiar.

I said, "Didn't I see you on the *Today* show the other morning?"

"Yes," he said modestly.

"When Al Roker went to the weather on the sidewalk in front of Radio City, weren't you the guy holding up a sign that read BUBBA FROM BUFFALO?"

"That was me. It's the first time anyone from Buffalo has been recognized in years. They are talking about having a parade for me when I get home."

"How did it happen?"

"Well, I was standing on the sidewalk with my sign when Al came out."

"Where did you get the sign?"

"My wife made it for me. She knew I was going to New York on business, so she said, 'Go to NBC. You're better-looking than most of the people on the show, and besides, it's Buffalo's turn.'"

"It might have been. Mark Russell comes from there," I said.

"I practiced several mornings. Then last Friday I decided to go for it. I arrived at six A.M. to get a good place. There were several people there already, and we shared coffee. But we knew as soon as Al came out it was every man and woman for himself or herself. I knew it would be tough. There was a Girl Scout troop from Omaha, a couple who were celebrating their fiftieth wedding anniversary, and the drum-and-bugle corps of USC."

I said, "You have to have a lot of talent to go up against them."

"Anyhow, I sized up the crowd and took my place next to six nuns from St. Mary's of Notre Dame. They were my toughest competition. I knew Roker would go to them, as he really likes to give anyone from Notre Dame a sound bite."

He continued, "The newspapers reported that I knocked over a schoolteacher from Salt Lake City to get to the head of the line. This is not true. She tripped when she pushed me."

"Then what happened?"

"Well, it was seven-thirty, and Al came out. There was a cheer from the crowd as he held his microphone up. As I guessed, he immediately started talking to the nuns. I figured he either would go to the left or to the right, so I yelled to get his attention. 'Al! I'm Bubba from Buffalo!' My wife said I read the line beautifully."

"Then Al followed up by asking, 'How is the weather in Buffalo?'

"I immediately replied, 'Sunny, with eight feet of snow.' This broke everyone up. Al didn't know when he chose me that I had such a good sense of humor."

"And now you are recognized wherever you go?"

"Celebrity isn't what everyone thinks it is. I can't go anywhere without people asking for my autograph. They think they're funny when I'm in a restaurant and they say, 'How's Bubba from Buffalo?'"

I asked him if he would do it again, and he said, "Yes, but this time I want to be paid for it."

Security vs. Freedom

THE BIG BATTLE IN AMERICA on the home front is security vs. freedom. What makes it so important now is that it affects the social status of every citizen in the country.

Gloucester, who is now in airport security, is a very happy man.

"I'm working class and I can tell the middle and upper class what to do or not do."

"In what respect?"

"I'm a security guard, and people have to obey anything I tell them. For example, despite their wealth and title, if I tell them they can't go through that door, they can't go through it. They have to go through the other door I tell them to, which is two miles away. If I make the passengers open up all their baggage, they have no choice. I don't make a lot of money, but I get a lot of respect."

"I should think so. The lower-income class must be having a ball feeling that power."

"We're better off than we have been in the past. Take underpaid doormen in apartment houses. They used to take a lot of guff from the tenants. Now doormen give out guff. You can't get upstairs in the elevator if they don't want you to."

"Do you need a lot of education to be in the security business?"

"You don't have to be a nuclear scientist to search the trunk of someone's car or spend twelve hours a day as the bodyguard of a movie star. I know guys who don't have a high-school education who are now searching in the mail for anthrax spores."

"Is there any difference between security people who wear uniforms and those who don't?"

"American women are much more attracted to guys in uniforms. Because of the war, they stand taller and look sharper. I know a guy who guards the pandas at the zoo. In the name of security, gals are crazy about him."

"What is the most important thing for someone in charge of keeping the home front safe?"

"First, I would say you have to have good feet. Most security people have to stand on their feet eight to twelve hours a day. Second, you must be prepared to shoot a suspicious person if he fits the FBI profile, and third, you must have a sense of humor."

"The Senate voted 100 to 0 to federalize security at airports. The House voted 286 to 139. What's the difference?"

"The House had information the Senate didn't have."

"Does being a security guard give you the perks that the upper class no longer have?"

"It certainly does. Where else but in America can you win the power struggle for seven dollars an hour?"

Rumors of War

WHEN A WAR STARTS, can rumors be far behind? Rumors are essential to a free society and can make or break the home front.

If you are going to be a rumor spreader, you have to play by the rules. First, you cannot circulate a rumor until it is confirmed by two sources. For example, suppose your brother-in-law says, "I hear the terrorists are going to strike when everyone is cutting their lawns."

If his friend Arnold confirms it, you may pass it on to a third person. Then it will appear on the talk shows, etc.

Let's take another rumor. "The Carlsons are breaking up after thirty years of marriage." It came from Sarah Beecham, who heard it from Jennifer Sloane. The rumor started at the hairdresser's, where almost all good rumors are given birth. It's passed on from hair blower to hair blower.

By the time it got to the manicure table, the rumor had Carlson dating a thirty-five-year-old meter maid and Mrs. Carlson dating a much younger man.

When I heard this, I felt it my duty to tell Richfield because he invests his money with Carlson in Boeing Aircraft.

In order to be passed on, the rumor has to have legs. I heard this one from Jane Merriweather, who heard it from the secretary of the head of a movie studio, who heard it from a stuntman: "Don't go to a shopping mall during any months with the letter R in them."

I know what you're asking. Suppose you're not sure whether a rumor is true or not. You may pass it along provided you heard it from a "reliable source," such as a gas station attendant, who heard it from a customer, who had a shotgun in his car.

One of the latest rumors, which has spread like wildfire, has to do with the new government dress code. The rumor was believed to have started in the Four Leaf Bar, where the FBI goes for happy hour.

The rumor is that very soon, FBI agents will not be wearing ties. Thus, they will fade into the crowd, and no one will know who they are.

I know it's difficult, if not almost impossible, for the crime busters to walk around without ties on. But this is war, and you have to have a disguise. The rumor also says the FBI spokesman will appear on TV in grungy, unpressed suits so the enemy won't know if he is a bad guy or a good guy.

To further the deception, the FBI can no longer wear the zip-up jackets with FBI written on the back. The only acceptable stencil to be worn on the backs of jackets is BIG BIRD.

The same rumor has it that FBI agents must wear tennis clothes and T-shirts so people won't spot them going in and out of the White House.

This is just a rumor, but remember, you heard it here first.

Another Scare

THE POST OFFICE IS ASKING for five billion dollars over their present budget because people are using the mail 10 percent less than before the postal scare.

Even the Laughlan family has become unnerved. Mark Laughlan came in from work and spied the mail on the hall table. His wife, Sue, took the mail into the kitchen. She picked up a letter, and Mark shouted, "Don't open it!"

"It's a birthday card from Grandma for Buzzie."

"Why would she send a birthday card?"

"For one reason, it's Buzzie's birthday, and she always puts five dollars in with the card."

"How do we know it's from Grandma?"

Sue said, "I know her handwriting."

"Suppose someone stole Grandma's birthday card from a mailbox and sprinkled it with you-know-what?"

Buzzie, their thirteen-year-old, came into the kitchen and said, "Is that birthday card for me?"

Sue said, "We don't know because your father won't let me open it."

Buzzie said, "She always sends me five dollars. Can't I get the money without the card?"

Mark answered, "It has to be unsealed, and I'm not doing that."

Buzzie said, "Uncle Harry said he sent me a present. Where is it?"

"It was tied with string, so I threw it in the trash dump."

"But it could be a baseball glove," Buzzie cried.

"Or a terrorist bomb."

Sue asked, "Mark, does this mean we can't open any mail?"

Mark replied, "You can still open junk mail."

"Why?"

"Terrorists don't stuff anything in junk mail because they know a lot of people throw it away without reading it."

"Suppose Grandma calls and asks me if I liked my birthday card?" Buzzie asked.

Mark replied, "Tell her you can't open it because you have to be vigilant."

Sue said, "I don't think she'll buy that. Why do we get any mail if we can't open it?"

"Because whoever is stuffing you-know-what in letters would want us to be afraid."

Buzzie complained, "I knew I wouldn't have a birthday."

The mail is now piling up in the Laughlan kitchen. The only good that has come of the mail scare is that Mark keeps writing to the gas company that "the check is in the mail." He figures they have to believe it whether they want to or not.

BEFORE SEPTEMBER 11, 2001

Part One

Will Bill Interfere?

FOR ALL ITS SOUTHERN CHARM, Washington can still be a bitchy town—particularly when a new administration is coming in.

Right now the tongues are wagging about how much influence Bill Clinton will have in the White House when his wife, First Lady Hillary Clinton, takes office.

Rumors have it that Clinton will try to take over and be in on all of Hillary's decisions. But this has been adamantly denied by close friends of the Clintons'.

One told me, "Bill Clinton will have no more influence on governing the country than Ronald Reagan did when Nancy Reagan was in power. The press has been constantly speculating about Bill's obsession with interfering, but that's not his style. He never got involved when Hillary ran things in Arkansas, and he is not about to now."

Another friend said, "It's unrealistic to think that when the Clintons retire at night Bill will not ask Hillary, 'What happened in the country today?' It would be foolhardy to assume that Hillary would hold back, except, of course, on national security matters. But you have to expect that sometimes Hillary will use Bill as a sounding board."

I spoke to a newspaperman from Little Rock and he said, "You're going to see the hand of Bill Clinton in everything Hillary does. When he was governor he promised to keep out of Hillary's politics, but, unlike what his friends claim, he never did. Bill is one of those husbands who like to meddle in things they don't understand."

"I guess the question everyone in Washington is asking is, 'How much will Hillary make use of Clinton?'" I said.

"Well, she's giving him his own office and secretary in the White House, and she has already announced that her door to the Oval Office will always be open to him. There is no doubt that Clinton will be given assignments such as representing Hillary at luncheons when she can't make it herself. She has also indicated that Bill will attend Cabinet meetings. There's nothing wrong with that. George Bush did it, and so did Jimmy Carter. Most First Ladies like to have someone around whom they can trust."

"People seem to be afraid that Bill Clinton may have his own agenda—unlike Ronald Reagan, who didn't have one. Will Hillary be as tough about moving forward as Nancy?"

"Every First Lady has a mandate from the American people, but you don't know until she takes over what she will do with it. Barbara Bush started out as a cuddly bear, but by the time the election rolled around she had turned into a man-eating tiger. Politics affects First Ladies like that."

Finally, I posed the big question to a director of the League of Women Voters: "Do you believe that a First Lady should serve more than two terms?"

"The League has not taken a position on that, but personally I feel that there should not be limits. There are some First Ladies who aren't worth two months and others who could easily serve a lifetime. I feel that if a First Lady knew she was going to be in for only eight years, she might not give it her all."

"I know that this is not an easy one, but if you were Hillary, what would be the first thing you'd ask President Clinton to do?"

"I would require him to accompany me on all my trips for the American public to see that he is not the ambitious, conniving person everyone in the media has made him out to be."

The Day of Chutzpah

THE PHONE HAS BEEN RINGING off the hook with calls from historians who want to know what I was doing on December 7, 1941. After the third query, it occurred to me that I was giving out information I could easily use myself.

This is what I was doing on the Day of Infamy, which my father always referred to as the Day of Chutzpah. There were five friends at the Forest Hills Bowling Alley in the borough of Queens in New York City.

They were Bob Markay, Arnie Alperstein, George Hankoff, Dick Zimmerman and myself. All of us were sixteen years old and, next to bowling, our major topics of conversation were Glenn Miller, college football and girls. We were weak in current events.

It was early in the afternoon. George was ready to bowl when someone yelled from the cash register.

"The Japs have bombed Pearl Harbor!"

Before we go any farther, I want to explain that none of us were "politically correct" in those days, and we called the Japanese "Japs." We called them a lot worse names when we heard that they had sunk the entire U.S. fleet in Hawaii.

You cannot imagine our shock when the news sank in.

I was going for a spare and missed it by two feet.

We gathered around the radio. Franklin Roosevelt came on the air and gave us the story. It was as if our father were telling us that a family member had died. When Roosevelt finished, we looked at one another in silence.

Arnie broke it when he said, "We'll beat the friggin' blank-blanks in two weeks."

Dick added, "It won't take that long. They don't have any oil."

"How do you know that?" I asked.

"It was in Walter Winchell's column," he replied. "Besides, they eat raw fish, and when we bottle up Tokyo Bay they'll starve to death."

Bob said, "I hope that the war isn't over before we get in. I wouldn't mind killing some Japs."

"It will be over by then. We'll probably be part of the occupation army and go to dances with geisha girls and have great parties in the emperor's palace."

I said, "Maybe the Japs did more damage to Pearl Harbor than Roosevelt is admitting."

"How can they do any damage? Their planes are made of rice paper. Have you ever seen anything manufactured in Japan that could fly? Don't forget that the U.S. has the best antiaircraft weapons in the world."

"Where did you hear that?" George wanted to know.

"I saw it in Marvel comics."

I declared, "We'll have them on their knees by Christmas. In the movies they're always falling down when it comes to hand-to-hand fighting."

We stood around discussing the military aspects of the sneak attack, as well as how our armed forces should respond. We weren't sure what measures Roosevelt ought to take, but we all agreed that we should teach the Japs a lesson they'd never forget.

(Little did we know that someday there would be nothing but Toyotas.)

We couldn't do anything until we had more information, so we went back to the lanes. Arnie bowled 209, George scored 198, Dick got a 183, and my score was 160. Whenever people have asked me what I thought of Pearl Harbor, I always tell the truth—I was bowled over.

Spray Me

IT'S HAPPENING MORE AND MORE. Whenever I go into a department store, I have to run the gauntlet of beautiful models spraying perfume at me. I feel as if I am being attacked with fragrant-smelling Mace.

These people do not work for the store but are employed by the various perfume houses who obviously hope that after having been doused with the perfume you'll buy barrels of it for a loved one, or use it to attract somebody who could be.

This is what took place the other day. I walked into the main entrance of Dumbold and Klein when a most attractive model yelled, "Stop, or I'll fill you full of Thinning Ozone."

"Don't shoot," I begged. "I'll do anything you want me to, providing it's almost within the law."

"I'm going to slosh your wrist, but I must warn you that Ozone has been known to drive men into fits of passion from which there is no return."

"Don't do it," I said. "I have an appointment with my dentist this afternoon, and he gets upset when I wiggle in the chair."

As the model raised her bottle, another young woman raced up with her flacon and sprayed me first.

The Ozone lady erupted in anger. "He was mine," she cried. "I had him in my atomizer as soon as he walked through the door."

"Baloney. He was standing in the neutral zone," the second young lady declared. "Anyone's fair game in the aisle next to the costume jewelry counter."

"What did you spray on me?" I demanded to know.

"It's called Designated Lover. The person who wears this will never have to go home alone."

"Don't believe her," the Ozone lady whispered. "Her perfume is made from recycled cabbage leaves. It will drive away the one you love."

The other saleslady said to her, "If Designated Lover wasn't the most costly perfume in the Western world, I'd spill it all over your panty hose."

I didn't know what would happen next. Then I looked around and saw eight beautiful women, all with tasseled atomizers, coming toward me. I was surrounded.

"Please," I pleaded. "Don't spray. My wife will never believe me when I explain to her why I smell like the Philadelphia Madam."

One lady said, "I'm going to spray Naked Panda on your earlobe. Tell me what you think."

"I can't hear you if you spray perfume in my ear," I told her. A model stepped forward holding a Gucci scarf. "What's that for?"

"We're going to put you against the wall and give you a smell test."

"Can I at least have a last cigarette?"

"Smoking is not allowed in the store."

I heard a voice say, "Ready, aim, fire."

A dozen squirts of perfume hit my face, my chest, and my arms. Only then did they take the blindfold off and allow me to buy a pair of socks, which is what I went into the store for in the first place.

Made in the U.S.A.

LIFE IS NOT ONLY UNFAIR — it's also more complicated. I am willing to avoid buying anything made abroad, but my problem is that I don't know what is a domestic product and what is foreign.

Recently a town in New York had to buy earthmovers. The choice was between John Deere earthmovers and Komatusu, a Japanese machine. There was an uproar when the town fathers were said to be considering Komatusu over Deere. John Deere finally won the contract. Only then was it revealed that Komatusu earthmovers were made in America and the John Deere ones were manufactured in Japan.

Once upon a time Lee Iacocca declared war on Japanese products because they were destroying the American automobile industry. He urged people to retaliate by boycotting Japan.

This was fine until it was discovered that the Dodge Stealth, one of Chrysler's better-selling models, was made by the Mitsubishi plant in Nagoya, Japan.

What is the patriotic consumer to do?

I went into a shopping mall to purchase a Star-Spangled Banner sweatsuit. The salesperson said that they had some from Hong Kong for $10, some from Taiwan for $15 and a few from Pakistan for $4.

"Don't you have any that were made in America?"

"No. The only American-made items we have are these Buddhist robes. They are hand-sewn in Lancaster, PA, by the Amish people."

I moved on to another store where I found athletic equipment, including Minnesota Indian Skis—made in Indonesia.

"Do you have any American skis?" I inquired.

The salesclerk replied, "We have these Kamakazi Slaloms that were manufactured in Minnesota."

"Why do American industries put foreign names on products that are made in this country?"

"Because they sell better. The U.S. consumer is used to buying products made abroad. American companies don't care what the items are called as long as they sell."

I went forth in search of anything made in the U.S.A.

I found a Baltimore Orioles baseball cap.

"Is this made in America?" I asked.

The salesperson replied, "The crown was made in Sicily, the band was made in Guadalcanal, and the peak was put on in Puerto Rico. That's what makes it American."

In another store I noticed a bowl of water with goldfish in it. "Those are nice fish," I remarked.

"They're just off the boat from the Yangtze River."

"I was hoping that they'd be from the U.S.A."

"We can't afford to carry American goldfish anymore—not since the Chinese flooded our shores with their own fish."

"That isn't very patriotic of you," I said.

"The U.S. is unable to compete against fish that are bred in slave-labor camps. The bowl was made in Poland, if it will make you feel any better."

"I have pledged to buy American no matter how difficult it is."

He pointed me in the direction of the U.S. Post Office. The man behind the counter said, *"Lo siento mucho. No hablo inglés."*

A Pill Collector

YEARS AGO THE BIG PROFITS in the United States were made in oil. These days they come from pharmaceuticals.

Pills cost so much that Americans are now buying them for investment rather than for curing an ailment.

Nick Nargosi is one of the major speculators in prescription drug trading and has made a fortune. He invited me over to his house to see his pill collection.

Two burly guards searched me and escorted me into Nargosi's ornate office.

He said, "Pill dealing was never much of a business in the past. People just took pills without thinking about their appreciating in value. They are now kicking themselves for not putting their prescriptions away in a safe."

He held up a pink capsule. "Take this diuretic, for example. Originally it was made for high blood pressure and cost twenty-five cents. If I sold it today, it would be worth twenty-five thousand. Of course, that's not all profit for me. The drug companies would get at least half."

"What's in that case over there?"

"That's a tranquilizer," Nick said. "Sotheby's sold one like it last week for eighteen thousand. It's a big item with pill collectors."

"How do you explain the surge in prescription drug prices in the last few years?"

"It's related to the price of cotton. As you know, all prescriptions come one part pill and five parts cotton. When the price of cotton went soaring, the manufacturers had no choice but to raise the cost of their drugs. I read in a prescription drug catalogue that you can get eight thousand dollars just for the cotton that comes in the bottles."

One of the guards brought out a velvet tray.

Nargosi picked up a magnifying glass from his desk.

"These are some of the crown jewels of prescription drugs. This green pill is made of aspirin and codeine. It was sold to us by an old lady on Medicare who found it when she was cleaning out her medicine cabinet. It was obvious that she had no idea of the value of the tablet and thought it had something to do with pain. The company that made it offered me eleven thousand to buy it back because they were planning to raise the price of it again."

He showed me a black-and-white capsule. "There are collectors all over the country who would kill for this muscle relaxer."

"How much is it?"

Nick laughed. "If you have to ask, you can't afford it."

"The drug companies say that they need to charge a lot of money and make unbelievable profits in order to stay in business," I said.

"They have to say that because people are starting to complain about the costs. The fact is that prescriptions are a risky gamble, and you shouldn't accept one from your doctor if you are going to complain about the bill."

The guard took away one tray and brought another.

"What are those?" I asked.

"They're over-the-counter drugs. Since prescription ones have gotten so expensive, many investors are now turning their attention to these. You can make a bonanza on them if you know what you're doing. This sugar-coated antacid pill was ten cents two years ago and is now worth twenty dollars. I don't sell them. I just keep them around to amuse my friends."

"Aren't you afraid of keeping so many valuable prescription drugs in your house?"

"Not really. Even if the thieves got inside, no one would be able to open the safety caps of the bottles."

Winner Take All

I WENT TO FLORIDA RECENTLY, and it could not have been at a more auspicious moment. A state lottery was being held, and the grand prize was $88 million, which, even in Florida, isn't chopped liver.

The tickets cost $1 each, and you had to pick six numbers to win. It wasn't hard to do, particularly if you had a strong background in remedial arithmetic. Although I hated to take that much money out of Florida, I bought twenty tickets on a hunch that fate had brought me there for that purpose.

We lottery players are a special breed. We believe that everything we do is dictated by chance—good luck and bad luck. Chance has not always been kind to us, and so we are certain that the only way we can recoup our misfortune is by striking it rich in a lottery. Some call us dreamers, but I prefer to think of us as positive thinkers who live from hand to mouth.

What makes playing the lottery so satisfying is that it gives us an opportunity to fantasize about what we'll do when we get the money.

In my case, I made up my mind that when I won I wouldn't change. I would still be the same happy-go-lucky, poker-faced gambler that I have always been. I'd continue to give my wife the same household allowance as before. I told her that we would still travel coach when visiting the children and that I would save shopping bags to use a second time.

The real fun of sweepstakes dreaming is how you will settle scores with people who haven't been very nice to you. Once your number is drawn, you know that they're going to come sucking around, trying to get their hands on your winnings.

There is this guy—I'll call him George—who always makes fun of my cheap clothes and complains that I am wearing the wrong tie. Well, just wait. When I win the big one I'm going to buy a $300 tie that doesn't match and wear it with a $2,500 suit that doesn't fit.

The beauty of America is that when you have $88 million, you can wear anything you want.

Shorty Lox is another one who gets nothing from me. He's always made fun of my past investments. What really tees me off is that he doesn't tell *me* how stupid I am; he tells my wife—and she always takes Shorty's word against mine. I expect that as soon as the news gets out about my windfall, Shorty will be at the door begging to know my secret of how I can pick six numbers out of the air and play tennis at the same time.

I'll probably give the kids a million or two, although I don't want them to get the idea that their father can win a lottery every day of the week. They should know that disappointment and heartbreak go with the system, and even the best of the lottery winners can stumble.

When you have a statewide lottery of these proportions, everyone expects to strike gold. I was talking to a lady at dinner about my winning the lottery, and the waiter interrupted us and said, "How can you win when I am going to win?"

Even the man handing out towels at the pool was certain that as soon as the numbers were drawn he could give up his job and buy himself a cabana in Hawaii and let somebody else bring him towels.

That's the way we lottery people are. With us, winning is like a religion. We always tell God we'll split the jackpot fifty-fifty if He helps us win.

It wasn't my turn last week, but it doesn't matter. There is a big sweepstakes coming up in New Jersey, and if I don't win that one there's always Puerto Rico.

Vacations Go to the Dogs

MANY PEOPLE HAVE NOT GONE on vacation this summer. It doesn't have to do with the economy. They can't leave because of their dogs.

Danzig said, "We wanted to go to the Berkshire Mozart Festival in the worst way but the hotel wouldn't take Moonrock, so we canceled."

"Why didn't you put Moonrock in a kennel?"

"We tried to do that last year, and he wouldn't look at us for four weeks. Alice said she wasn't going to go through that again."

I said, "Has it ever occurred to you that Moonrock is manipulating you and wants to be the center of attention? You should be firm and tell him that you two have a right to a vacation alone."

"You don't know Moonrock. If I told him that, he would get hurt and eat the rug. He doesn't even like it when we go to the movies and leave him home."

"The dog is running your life, " I told Danzig. "You should tell him that he either behaves like a grown-up or you'll give him away."

"We couldn't do that."

"Moonrock wouldn't know it was an idle threat. The important thing to understand is that you can have a dog wagging his tail some of the time and some of the tail wagging a dog all of the time. But you can't have all of the dog wagging his tail all of the time. We once had a dog named Zenith who terrorized us. We couldn't go anywhere without him howling into the night. 'All right,' we told him, 'if you want to go out so badly you go out and we'll stay at home.' We put Zenith out in the backyard several nights, and when he realized we were practicing tough love he stopped howling."

"Alice would never let me do that. She says she knows what is going on in Moonrock's head. He's thinking, 'How much can they love me if they want to put me in a kennel in the summertime?'"

"Some of the best dogs in town go to kennels in August."

"And some of the worst ones, too. A dog may be man's best friend, but he is not another dog's best friend. Alice says she could never enjoy Mozart knowing Moonrock was being fed by a stranger."

I told Danzig, "You're good dog owners. But you can't sit at home in the heat because of a pet. You have to think of yourselves and say, 'It isn't as if we haven't done everything in our power to take Moonrock with us. How much more does he want?'"

"That's easy for you to say. But last year we wanted to go to Maine, and Moonrock was so upset he ate two feet of the couch."

"What did you do?"

"We canceled the trip. We felt this was Moonrock's way of telling us that if we left he was going to eat the whole house."

"It's your dog, and you can do what you want."

"We want to go to the Berkshires for the Mozart Festival. But we have to live with Moonrock all year, and we only have to live with Mozart for a week. Maybe you could take Moonrock for us."

I was aghast. "You have to be crazy. Who wants to board somebody else's dog?"

"I thought you'd say that. People are always talking about how
much they love other people's pets. But when push comes to
shove, they won't even give them a bath."

Mr. President, Jr.

"WHAT DO YOU WANT TO BE when you grow up?" I asked little
Clem Maple.

He eyed me suspiciously, as eleven-year-olds tend to do, and
replied, "President of the United States."

"That's wonderful," I said. "What makes you think that you
could be president?"

"I can beat up every kid in my class."

"That isn't exactly a qualification."

"My daddy says it is. He claims that if you can't beat up everybody in your class, you don't have what it takes to run in an election."

"I guess there is something to that. But there's more to being
president than fighting dirty. You must be able to answer the
tough questions that the press will throw at you. For example,
have you ever smoked pot?"

"No."

"Not even once when you were waiting to go out on the field
for Little League baseball?"

"No, I never did."

"What about women? Are there any in your life who might pop up at the time you are running for election? Level with me, because Americans hate political surprises."

"I don't know any women. I know a girl named Anne-Marie Dunn in my class, but I only kissed her once because she has braces on her teeth and she cut my lip."

"In order to be president of the United States you will have to raise a great deal of money. Are you prepared to do this?"

"I don't know."

"Well, think about it. You must make deals with many organizations in exchange for their political-action contributions. There's nothing wrong with it because all politicians are nice to the person who gives them money."

"How do I do that?"

"Invite the big givers to the White House, call them by their first names and make sure that no legislation is passed to offend them."

"Is that what a president does?"

"On his good days. On his bad days he vetoes bills that he thinks could save the grizzly bear. By the way, if you are elected president, are you prepared to blame Congress for everything that has gone wrong in the country?"

"I don't know."

"Well, you had better decide. No president can defend his own record without blaming Congress for theirs. Clem, you shouldn't dream of being president unless you have a game plan. Did you ever try to get out of serving in the Vietnam War?"

"What's the Vietnam War?"

"Never mind. Are you for a balanced budget?"

"I am not sure."

"Well, you can't run for the White House without promising a balanced budget and a prayer in every school."

"I don't know if I want to be president of the United States anymore."

"What do you want to be?"

"A star hockey player. Then all you have to do is hit people with a stick."

Murder, She Said

THIS COULD BE CALLED "The Year of the Killing Fields." It seems that everyone has a reason to kill somebody in order to save somebody else.

I was walking past an abortion clinic when a "right-to-lifer" ordered me to choose sides. He said that if I were against the "lifers," he would kill me.

"That's a hostile attitude, particularly since you are in the business of saving human beings."

"Pro-choice people are not human beings. They are murderers and should get the death penalty."

I explained to the man that while I didn't agree with what he said, I would defend to the death his right to say it, as long as he would do the same for me.

He said, "Forget it."

"Look," I told him, "I happen to be a friend of both Roe and Wade, and I am sure that they would not approve of you setting fire to clinics that legally perform abortions."

He responded, "That's how much you know. Neither Roe nor Wade condoned murder. If we don't prevent this carnage, who will?"

"But you can't kill people to save them," I said. "You are telling women what to do with their bodies even though your sex got them into this mess in the first place."

At this point a pro-choice lady came up and yelled, "If you care so much about life, why are you trying to kill everyone?"

"Why don't you drop dead!" the antiabortion protester shouted back.

"I have no intention of dropping dead, but I'll destroy anyone who tries to close down this clinic."

I didn't realize how heated this debate could become. The pro-choice woman was sticking her finger in the right-to-lifer's chest. "This is not a question of life or death—it's one of choice. Those of us who want to keep abortion legal are not murderers, but we are willing to die for what Roe believed in."

Neither side seemed to be getting anywhere, so I strolled over to the Supreme Court.

A large group was marching in a circle protesting the execution of convicted murderer Robert Alton Harris. One sign proclaimed: DEATH TO THE GOVERNOR OF CALIFORNIA; another read, CAPITAL PUNISHMENT IS CRUEL AND UNUSUAL AND SO IS THE SUPREME COURT; another just said, MURDER MOST FOUL.

The capital punishment group a few feet away was yelling things like "Take gas," and, "Pull the switch," and, "If he can't feel it, it isn't punishment."

The two groups were screaming at each other, and both gave the impression that none of them would settle for anything less than first-degree homicide. The pro-gas-chamber demonstrators were demanding the castration of their opponents.

I tried to put my two cents in.

"I speak for the voices of sanity," I said, holding my arm in the air like Mahatma Gandhi. "We should be nice to each other."

Both sides started to pelt me with vegetables.

"Go back to where you came from," someone shouted.

"Are you crazy?" I yelled. "I just came from an antiabortion rally."

The Final Test

THERE IS A SIMPLE SOLUTION to the controversy over the war records of Bill Clinton and Dan Quayle. The two are accused of having used political influence to stay out of the hostilities in Indochina.

The way to solve it is that instead of debating the issue over and over again in some clammy network studio, both Clinton and Quayle should go to Vietnam, in full uniform, and show the American public if they really have the right stuff.

The plan would be to take the two men into the mountains around Khe San and assign each one a hill to capture. They would do this alone without aid from the Green Berets or the 82nd Airborne.

To make sure the public witnessed the action, CNN would cover it live.

Before going into battle, each man would have a half hour on the Larry King show to profess his patriotism for the United States and his love of the military.

I know some people are saying, "Isn't it a little late to go to Vietnam?" The answer is obvious to anyone running for public office: "Better late than never."

To make sure that the idea was viable, I made some telephone calls.

The first one was to Hanoi asking if they had any objection to Clinton and Quayle coming over and taking a few hills to help them in the presidential campaign.

The official wanted to know if I was out of my blinkin' mind. He said, "If they were chicken then, we don't want them now."

I told him, "Our election depends on it. You must allow them in."

"Why?"

"Because you owe us. You have a lot of hills. All we're asking is that you let Quayle and Clinton take two of them."

"Okay, but we don't want you to start making a habit of this every time you hold an election."

I then called Governor Clinton's top aide. "Good news. I've fixed it so that the governor can still go to Vietnam."

"Governor Clinton doesn't believe in the war."

"Nobody does, but it has become a campaign issue, and the only way you can deal with it is to have him go over and hang a coonskin on the wall."

"Has Quayle agreed to this?" Clinton's man asked.

"I've got a call in to him right now. Anyone who won his battle stars in Indianapolis should be dying to visit Saigon."

"If he goes, then our man will go."

I called the Quayle brain trust. "Is Quayle willing to go to Vietnam and take a hill to prove that he's not a coward?"

"That's a hypothetical question."

"It's not hypothetical. It's all laid out. The Vietnamese say that it's okay with them, providing that Clinton and Quayle leave the hills the way they found them."

"Will there be any Vietnamese opposition?"

"Not much. Just enough to prove that both candidates are willing to fight for their country."

The Quayle staffer said, "You know, the vice president was in public relations in the National Guard. He doesn't know too much about taking hills."

I responded, "America will match one National Guard PR man against ten Viet Cong any day of the week."

Kidnapping Made Easy

I AM NOT ONE OF THOSE PEOPLE who are always criticizing a Supreme Court decision—but every once in a while I wonder if the justices' elevators really go to the top floor.

The Court's 6-to-3 decision on kidnapping is a case in point. The Supremes ruled that it was legal for the United States to kidnap someone in a foreign country to bring him or her back for trial without the approval of the nation whose borders have been violated.

As a hard-liner I am not disturbed about the United States violating international law, particularly if the person kidnapped is guilty. What troubles me is that the people doing the kidnapping are prone to make mistakes, and you may wind up with a number of foreigners being snatched who have nothing to do with any American crimes.

I will give you an example.

"Ricardo Alvarez, we are American agents and we have been ordered to drug you, put you in chains and drag you back to the United States to stand trial for murder, for using a false credit card at a Taco Hut, and for speeding in Arizona."

"My name is not Alvarez. It is Alacazar."

"Alvarez, Alacazar—they both have one *l*. Trust us. We don't make mistakes."

"But you have the wrong man. Alvarez lives in the next block. He weighs two hundred and ninety pounds. I weigh one hundred and forty pounds."

"It isn't for us to decide if we have the wrong man or not. When we get you over the border we will assign you a lawyer, and it will be his job to prove you are a victim of mistaken identity. It says right here on our kidnap authorization slip that our man lives at two-three-four Simon Bolivar Lane. That is this house."

"But this is two-three-four Simon Bolivar Boulevard. Are you going to take me from my family?"

"You should have thought of that before you illegally shipped three hundred pounds of fireworks to your cousin on Long Island for his daughter's wedding."

"By what authority can you kidnap me from my own country?"

"By authority of the Supreme Court of the United States, whose justices have declared that no one is safe from the long arm of the law. Come with us, Mr. Alvarez."

"Alacazar, my name is Alacazar."

"If you're going to be picky-picky about your name, we're not going to let you plea-bargain for a lighter sentence."

Although this type of behavior bothers me, what really has me distressed is that if the Supremes say we can kidnap foreign citizens, what is to prevent foreign agents from snatching our citizens?

"Mr. Smith, we are from the Mexican secret police. Please step into this coffin so we can take you back to Guadalajara for trial as a war criminal."

"I have never been to Guadalajara."

"Several people have identified you as Ivan the Terrible."

"My name isn't Ivan."

"Alacazar's name wasn't Alvarez either, yet they took him anyway."

"But I am an American citizen, and we're in Santa Monica, California."

"We can't help it. Your Supreme Court has made it a jungle out there."

Charge Me

REJOICE, ALL YOU CONSUMERS — Big Brother has gone into the credit card business. It has been revealed that American Express not only signs customers up for credit cards but also sells the information on their spending habits to other organizations. These companies pay a nice sum to get the dope on a person's lifestyle for use in their marketing business.

Under pressure from New York State, Amex agreed to notify its twenty million cardholders that it does compile profiles of them, which it then "rents" out.

But it has agreed to take a customer's name off the list if he or she begs them to.

I must say that when I heard what Amex had been doing I was terribly worried. I thought that my buying habits were privileged information and that the less people knew about my lifestyle the better off I was.

My imagination went wild.

"Hello, American Express? This is the Tearduct Department Store. What have you got on A. Buchwald of Washington, D.C.?"

"Just a minute. Here it is on the computer. He buys cheap shoes."

"We suspected that. Anything else?"

"He wears smudged eyeglasses. He only cleans them once every other week. He buys Edge shaving cream, Crest toothpaste and Mitchum deodorant. He buys one stick every three weeks, so we assume that he perspires more than the average media person."

"Anything about his love life?"

"This year he bought a dozen Valentine cards at a Hallmark store in Santa Monica, California, so we guess that he's quite a swinger."

"And sports?"

"We show that he purchased a can of tennis balls in 1988 but hasn't bought one since. This could either mean he has given up the game or found a way to come out on the court empty-handed. We suspect the latter."

"Will you bring up what you have on his dining habits?"

"He loves to eat and will spare no expense to stuff himself. His last restaurant bill indicates that he had baked lasagna, linguini, roast duck and crème caramel, with a bottle of expensive Château Talbot Bordeaux. He gave the waiter a fifteen percent tip and the captain ten. He also bought a stuffed panda for the lady he was with, which cost fifty dollars, and it was charged to his card."

"The pieces of the puzzle are starting to fill in. What about his health?"

"We're in luck. He paid his doctor's bill with his American Express card. The man is overweight and is getting deaf. I would target him for a hearing aid pitch. His doctor gave him an over-the-counter prescription for poison ivy, and it cost him a hundred and twenty-three dollars at the drugstore."

"So far his profile fits our needs. The man is a natural for a new living-room furniture suite."

"Hey, wait a minute. Something just came up on the screen. It says that Buchwald has received four parking tickets in the last eight months. He paid them with his American Express card but failed to add a tip for the meter maid."

"We get the picture. Give us his unlisted telephone number, and we'll turn it over to our junk phone call department. He'll go crazy trying to figure out how we got through to him."

Dinner Is Served

THEY HELD A DEMOCRATIC FUND-RAISER in Washington the other night. For as little as $15,000 a table you could eat in the same hall as the president-elect and Mrs. Clinton.

Democratic bigwigs insisted that those who came to the affair were not trying to buy access to the new president and his administration but were investing in a movement to change America for the better. That's why so many Republican lobbyists attended.

"Why do Washingtonians turn up for political fund-raisers?" I asked some influence peddlers.

One man replied, "These dinners are a good buy. For fifteen hundred per person you get soup, a fish course, a good slice of roast beef and a vegetable, plus a salad and baked Alaska for dessert. I defy you to find a meal at that price anywhere else in Washington, except at Scholl's Cafeteria."

I asked Pat Kilroy, a female lobbyist, why she was there. "No woman lobbyist can get into the locker room at the Burning Tree Country Club, so we come here for our male bonding," she told me.

Everyone I talked to denied that he or she had bought a table to get in good with the president and his people.

One antienvironment lobbyist explained, "We would never do such a dumb thing. Democrats don't respect you if you buy tickets to their affairs in hopes of persuading them to support your cause. I'm here because I'm Al Gore's biggest fan, and I'll go anywhere if I know he'll be at the dinner."

I asked another lobbyist if he had bought any tickets for Republican fund-raisers recently.

"No," he admitted. "That's because the quality of the food has been falling off lately, and I find the service appalling. If you can't get a good fresh piece of chicken at a fund-raiser, then there's no reason to attend."

"What do people who come to fifteen-hundred-dollar-a-table dinners talk about?" I wanted to know.

A lobbyist for the Meatpackers of America said, "We talk about the same things that most Americans talk about around the holidays—tax reform, unfair industry regulations, tariffs on Japanese and French imports and why we still need a strong military-industrial complex."

"I assume that there's no attempt to bring up any political problems that your clients may be experiencing."

"That would be very gauche. After all, when you dine in a man's house, you're there to enjoy yourself and have a good time. The only thing you might do is jump up between the meat and the dessert courses, shake hands with the president and say, 'Joe Flounder, Wallpaper Boosters Association.' So at least he knows you bought a table," a veteran lobbyist said.

I decided to pose another question to the group. "What about the people who can't afford fifteen thousand for a table?"

A fund-raiser chairman assured me that their voices would be respected the same as those supping inside.

"We have set aside sidewalk space in front of the White House and the Capitol for people who have a message. They'll need to shout it, but they will be heard."

"Will lobbyists have as much influence under the Democrats as they did under the Republicans?"

"Why not? We're all family."

Pardon Me

WHILE MANY WERE CHOSEN to fill President-Elect Clinton's top administration slots, others for various reasons fell by the wayside.

One was Sam Greengrass, who was on the short list for a Cabinet position. He actually was a shoo-in until he was interviewed by Clinton himself.

"What would it take," Clinton asked, "for you to accept an appointment?"

Greengrass replied, "A presidential pardon."

"A pardon? You haven't done anything to need a pardon."

"Not yet, but I have four years ahead of me, and I want to make sure that if I lie to Congress you'll back me up."

Clinton said, "I'll be honest with you. I haven't given that much thought to presidential pardons. Mr. Bush is still president, and I don't want to interfere with his powers. Besides, I hope to run a White House where it is not necessary to hand out pardons at the end of my term."

"If you don't mind my saying so, Mr. Clinton, that's wishful thinking. There hasn't been an administration yet where people, in order to protect the president or themselves, did not get into serious trouble. That is what democracy is all about. If I can keep my crimes from leading into the Oval Office, the least you can do is keep me out of Leavenworth."

"The problem with your request is that if word got out that I guaranteed you a pardon before you started, people might be waiting for you or me to do something crooked and obscene."

Greengrass said, "I won't leak it. It will be between you and me. For example, if we make a deal to give nuclear weapons to El Salvador in exchange for Mexican drug hostages, my lips will be sealed."

"I have no intention of doing that."

"Well, if you change your mind, I'll take the Fifth Amendment when I testify in front of Congress. But I have to know that if they pursue me that I won't stand trial."

"Greengrass, I want you in my Cabinet, but your price is high. No other appointee has asked for a pardon in advance."

"They haven't been around Washington long enough. A pardon is like a prenuptial agreement. It makes it clear what can and cannot be expected of the parties. I hope I will never have to ask for one—but an appointee never knows. Look at Cap Weinberger. Do you think in his wildest dreams he ever thought he would have to beg Bush for a pardon? I am not just worried about going to jail. What scares the heck out of me are the legal fees. When you screw up in the government, defense lawyers don't come cheaply."

The president-elect said, "I'm going to have to take this one up with Hillary. If I give you a pardon, I will be forced to give everyone in my administration one. It's a bad precedent."

"You're the boss, but I'm not going to put my neck on the line without a guarantee that if I mess up I have a presidential safety net."

"What could you possibly do for me that would get you in trouble?"

"I could order a search for your mother's passport application. That would be a felony."

"Okay, I'll think it over," Clinton replied. "If I agree, do you still want to work for me?"

"It's okay until something on the Supreme Court pops up. But first I better shred my notes on this conversation."

Hugging Never Hurt

I AM FINDING OUT THINGS about President-Elect Clinton very slowly. I attended a gathering at Hilton Head over the holidays. Once a year some of the finest minds in America gather on this East Coast island to solve the problems of the world and define the future for all mankind. This "Renaissance Weekend" could be called a coed Bohemian Grove.

Which brings me to President-Elect Clinton. I had a chance to study him at close hand. I was as near to him on one occasion as you are to the book you are now reading. Here's what I found out:

Our future president is a hugger. He hugs everybody—men, women, children, waiters, busboys and even the golden arches at McDonald's.

Most people sidle up to him timidly, hoping to get nothing more than a handshake. Instead, Mr. Clinton sweeps the well-wisher up into his arms and squeezes the breath out of him until the other person cries "uncle."

Anyone is entitled to a hug from Mr. Clinton, even if the person voted for Ross Perot.

One evening I was heading for the bar with Doug Marlette, the incorruptible cartoonist for *Newsday*, when he disappeared. I turned to his wife and said, "Where's Doug?"

She replied, "He's being hugged by the president."

The worst thing in the world for a political cartoonist is to be co-opted by a president. Once he is engulfed in the president's arms, he is compromised for life. When Doug returned, he was shaken, and his face had turned white. I tried to get by him but he just grabbed me.

"I'm so ashamed," he said.

"You're full of it, Doug," I told him. "You liked it. Why don't you admit that you would rather be hugged by Clinton than win a Pulitzer Prize?"

"How come he didn't hug you?" Doug asked.

"Because I climbed out a back window and he didn't see me."

Jim Freedman, the president of Dartmouth College and a serious historian of note, said, "We're going to have a lot of hugging in this administration—even more than under Lyndon Johnson. Bill Clinton is the first president we've had since Andrew Jackson who could hug and jog at the same time."

I asked Mr. Freedman if he thought that hugging would be part of Clinton's foreign policy.

"There is no doubt that it will be one of his key foreign strategies. Once Mr. Clinton puts his arms around the Japanese prime minister and holds him tight, the prime minister will say, 'Well, it's better than what Bush did to me.'"

"Do you envision a hugging match between Boris Yeltsin and Bill Clinton?"

"Very easily. Historically, the Russians have been the greatest huggers in the world, but when Clinton and Yeltsin hug each other, put your money on the American."

Freedman felt that if there is any trouble over diplomatic hugging it will be with France. François Mitterand has said on many occasions, "France may hug others but reserves the right to be hugged in return."

Finally I posed the question that everyone was dying to ask: "Should Bill Clinton hug George Bush on Inauguration Day immediately after he is sworn in?"

Freedman replied, "Only if Bush laughs."

The First Eight Days

A TV REPORTER SHOVED a microphone into my face last week and asked, "How do you think President Clinton is doing in his first eight days?"

I was reluctant to reply because I always write an in-depth piece on a president's first eight days. So I just said that his administration was an utter failure and President Clinton should resign and turn over the running of our country to the able Al Gore.

Instead of the reporter leaving it at that, he kept pressing me as to why Clinton had failed to live up to the promise that 43 percent of the country had for him.

I responded, "His inexperience showed up as soon as he took office. He didn't even know that the attorney general's baby-sitter

needed a green card. Do you know why? They don't have any illegal Peruvian aliens in Arkansas."

The man kept shoving the microphone down my throat. He
said, "But most attorney generals' baby-sitters don't have green
cards. That isn't enough to impeach a president."

"His foreign policies have been a failure. Look at Serbia,
Bosnia, Somalia and Israel. Nothing has changed in the last eight
days. And shall I tell you the reason? It's because Hillary Clinton
is not interested. If the First Lady isn't curious about foreign
affairs, why should the president be?"

The reporter accidentally wrapped the mike wire around my
neck. "People say what bugs them the most is that in just over a
week the president has been unable to balance the budget. Do
they have a right to be upset?"

"Yes, they do. Many mornings at dawn when the voters assumed
that Clinton was in his office working on the deficit, television
showed him out jogging with his Secret Service men. We didn't
elect a part-time president."

I thought we were finished, but the reporter persisted.

"How would you rate Socks the cat in the first eight days?"

"The cat is the only bright spot so far. Many people predicted
that he could never take the place of the Bushes' dog, Millie, but
he has surprised everyone. He is quiet and willing to listen. The
president's office is open to him at all times. He's not one of
those White House cats who bother President Clinton unless it is
absolutely necessary. Socks's main virtue is that he refuses to talk
to the press."

"As soon as Clinton's seven-day honeymoon was over, the public turned on him. Is that par for American voters?"

"He's lucky he had seven days. Until Mr. Clinton gets a Desert Storm under his belt, he is going to be criticized for all his domestic and foreign programs. Even the Democratic congress, one of the most agreeable legislative bodies in the land, is concerned about the eight days that Clinton has squandered so far."

I sensed that the interview was almost over because the reporter moved his knee out of my stomach. "How do you think President Clinton can save himself during the rest of his one thousand four hundred twenty-two days in office?"

"Get rid of the saxophone."

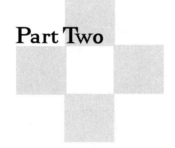

Part Two

Matchmaking in Washington

A WASHINGTON LAWYER FRIEND of mine whose name is Michael Spekter called me in the middle of the night and said excitedly, "What do you think of this? I've been reading up on the new attorney general appointee, Janet Reno, who maintains that she doesn't have a 'nanny' problem because she has no children.

"Listen to this. She's got guts. She has integrity and doesn't take any stuff from anybody. Furthermore, she was a great state's attorney, she's single and she has a mind of her own.

"There's more. She lived in a rustic cabin with her aged mother in the Everglades. Ms. Reno is crazy about the outdoors and enjoys hiking and canoeing and bird-watching."

I said, "Get to the point, Michael. It's one o'clock in the morning."

"Everyone agrees that she isn't as neat as a pin, but on the other hand she's not in favor of the death penalty nor is she pro-life—yet she follows the law."

"So?"

"I've been doing a computer search for a mate for her all evening, and I think that I've come up with the perfect match—Supreme Court Justice David Souter."

"You're crazy, Michael."

"Hear me out. Justice Souter lived alone in a house that he had rebuilt himself in New Hampshire with his aged mother.

"He likes hiking and nature and the outdoors. I couldn't find out if he was neat or not, but from what I've seen I wouldn't put him on any 'best-dressed' list. He has a mind of his own and has come to many decisions that Ms. Reno agrees with, much to the horror of the conservatives on the court. What makes it an incredible situation is that they are both single."

"You've done your homework, Michael, but where are you going with all this?"

"I don't think it's a coincidence that Ms. Reno was selected. I believe that Hillary is behind it. Perhaps she persuaded Bill to appoint someone to the Justice Department who had the same resume as a Supreme Court justice."

"It's an interesting match—so let's just follow through on it. Suppose Souter and Reno face each other in the court, their eyes lock and it's love at first sight. Then they get married. You know what something like that could lead to?"

"Kids."

"Right, and what do kids lead to?"

"Souter and Reno need a nanny in order to fulfill their duties," Michael said. "Like most Americans, they can't find one with a green card. I have a solution. They hire an illegal nanny and they get President Clinton to pardon her."

"That could work. What do you plan to do with all this match-making material?"

"I thought that you might plant it in the paper. It would give Souter and Reno something to think about."

"But they both like to live alone," I pointed out. "Won't match-making spoil their fun?"

"They could still be alone. They could alternate between New Hampshire and the Everglades and read each other's briefs."

"You've done wonderful work," I told Michael.

"I'll send it up the Justice Department flagpole and see who salutes."

Retraining for All

ONE OF PRESIDENT CLINTON'S PRIORITIES is to have a job-retraining program to get people back to work. So far, Mr. Clinton hasn't mentioned what kinds of jobs he wants to retrain people for.

There is one pilot program that has had some success. It's called the Here Today Gone Tomorrow Retraining Foundation. Larry Fluger, the executive director, assured me that Clinton has pledged to retrain forty million people for new careers.

"What exactly do you have in mind for those who were laid off in the auto industry?" I asked Larry.

"We're training them to become TV anchormen. Our research indicates that anchormen are some of the highest-paid people in this country, and hardly any intelligence is required. It's much easier to read a TelePrompTer than it is to weld a door onto an Oldsmobile."

"What other jobs are you retraining people for?"

"We're taking everyone in the defense industries and teaching them to be basketball stars. This country can never get enough good basketball players."

"Doesn't it take some knowledge of the game?"

"Less than it does to paint the flaps on a Stealth bomber. Workers in defense industries are never going to hit it big. But one contract with Nike and you're on easy street for the rest of your life.

"You see that room over there? Those people are being trained to be political pollsters. There will always be a need for people to poll the electorate. Most of the pollsters used to be in the CIA and are now out of a job. We're planning to train at least ten million before the next election."

"Someone has to see this to believe it," I said.

"Down there in the gymnasium we're retraining garment workers to become heart surgeons. Our studies show that the need for heart surgery will increase substantially over the next ten years, and if we can teach four or five million workers how to perform a triple bypass, our investment will pay off."

"Do you ever find a garment worker who just doesn't seem to have what it takes to be a heart surgeon?"

"If someone doesn't work out as a surgeon, we retrain him to be the head of a Hollywood movie studio. You don't need *any* brains for that."

"I imagine that as the economy continues to decline the retraining program will get bigger."

Fluger said, "Clinton has vowed to retrain every last person in this country who is out of work. He's left the details of how to do it to us.

"We also have a program to retrain all the politicians who lost in the election."

"What will you do with them?"

"We're going to turn them into lobbyists. They don't have to get their hands dirty, and it pays better than McDonald's."

War Games

IT'S ONE THING FOR PRESIDENT CLINTON to order American planes to bomb the bad Serbs in Bosnia—it's another for our military to actually do it.

This was quite clear when Navy pilots were given a briefing the other day aboard the aircraft carrier *Frostbite*.

Commander Chip English was in charge of the pointer. "This is a map of our target. We are going into Bosnia-Herzegovina at five hundred feet and knock the Bosnian Serbs back into the Stone Age. Any questions?"

"Sir, why the red strip on the map?"

"That's where the Croats and Muslims live. Under no circumstances are we to bomb them. All we're aiming at are Bosnian Serbs. That means lay off Yugoslav Serbs, even though we know they are egging on the Bosnian Serbs."

"Got it, sir. We just hit Bosnian Serbs and let it go at that."

"Exactly," said Commander English. "But make sure that you don't strafe any Macedonians who are fleeing the Albanians."

"Commander, is there any way for us to know the difference between the Serbs and the Muslims?"

"The Serbs are Eastern Orthodox and will be wearing crucifixes around their necks. You will encounter the most difficulty near Sarajevo, which has a mix of Serbs and Bosnians. Bomb the hills but stay away from the town unless someone fires at you.

"Did I mention the Croats? The Croats are all over Bosnia. They moved there centuries ago when Bosnia recruited Croats for their soccer teams. We don't want you to bomb Croats instead of Serbs because we need the Croats as a buffer once the peace treaty is signed. At the moment, the Croats are in league with the Serbs to ethnically cleanse the Bosnians. This does not mean we can drop anything on them willy-nilly."

"Commander, can you tell me what this war is all about?"

"No one is quite sure," English admitted. "One intelligence source reports that in 1312 a Serbian sheep strayed into a Bosnian Muslim field and the Bosnian farmer refused to return it. So the Serb kidnapped the Bosnian's daughter and made her marry his son. As a result, the Bosnians postponed the war they were fighting at the time with Croatia over fourth-class mailing privileges and attacked Belgrade. Then they went back to Sarajevo and got drunk on slivovitz.

"While the Bosnians got drunk, the Serbs attacked from the north and Greece attacked from the south. The rest is history. That more or less is the genesis of the dispute, which to this day hasn't been settled by the United Nations."

Commander English continued, "It's not our job to figure out the causes of this situation. Our mission is to stop those who continue to slaughter innocent people, and make sure that they pay the piper."

A pilot said, "Suppose we miss our target, sir. Can we go on and bomb Baghdad?"

"Out of the question. We have no proof that Saddam Hussein has any designs on Bosnia, although he could always use what the Serbs are doing in Sarajevo as an excuse to attack Kuwait again. Any other questions?"

"Suppose we get to our targets and the Serbs have moved all their guns out. Can we bomb Serbs in Hungary?"

"No, you can't. The only Serbs you are permitted to hit are those in Bosnia-Herzegovina. If you're not sure of your target, dump your bombs on Albania.

"I guess that winds it up. This mission is a piece of cake. Any of you should be able to do it with your eyes closed which, incidentally, might not be a bad idea."

Live a Little

"THEY DON'T TELL YOU the real truth about health care in this country," Peter Connole told me. "The reason health care costs so much is that people don't want to die."

I said, "That's a given, but I don't understand what it's got to do with the spiraling costs of medicine."

"In days gone by, Americans did not have the option. They just died at home or on the golf course, and everyone at the funeral parlor agreed that it was 'God's will.' Nowadays citizens insist on staying alive no matter what it costs the taxpayers."

"I guess you can't blame them."

"The truth is," Connole continued, "that the medical profession hasn't failed us. If anything, it's too successful. Physicians can perform miracles to keep someone breathing until that person is in his or her nineties. Just watch Willard Scott on the *Today* show when he announces someone's hundredth birthday. He used to spend all week digging up five candidates. Now he has thousands to choose from. This all comes from medical breakthroughs, and someone has to pay for them."

"Meaning you and me?"

"Will you allow a loved one to go to heaven when you know that Blue Cross can save him?"

"No. But as I see it, those who can afford the medical insurance get to live and those who can't pay will never make it to the *Today* show. Clinton wants to make sure that all people have access to life, liberty and the pursuit of senior-citizen discounts on airplanes."

"I thought that with greater volume costs would go down, but in this country the price keeps going up."

Connole explained, "That's because in order to keep someone alive it takes a much larger team. In the past when everyone said bye-bye at sixty-five, one doctor and one nurse were involved. These days hundreds of people are present—from skilled surgeons to the hospital cooks who prepare your salt-free meals. All these folks have to be compensated for their expertise because each of them plays a role in keeping the patient alive. That's where the money goes—that and the profits hospitals make on their parking lots."

"So every time we see Willard Scott announcing someone's hundredth birthday it's going to cost all of us."

Connole nodded. "The greatest mistake the country made was to develop lifesaving methods for the population without setting aside the funds for their continued care. What I resent is that Hillary and her gang of three thousand four hundred health experts won't level with the public. They should warn everyone that if medical advances continue at this pace, nobody is going to die and nobody will be able to pay for everyone's upkeep."

"There must be a better solution to the problem than that. Maybe Willard Scott could hold a telethon every morning and people could pledge money to keep everyone breathing, or perhaps we could have a surcharge tax for anyone who lives past eighty-five."

Connole said, "I would rather open gambling casinos in hospital wards and let the winnings pay for people's medical care. We would have slot machines in the halls all the way to the operating room. The most important thing that Hillary has to do now is tell the American people that there is no such thing as a free heart transplant on the Willard Scott show."

On the Street

ONE OF THE SADDEST SIGHTS in a big city is a group of smokers standing outside their office buildings puffing away because they are no longer permitted to smoke inside.

No people on earth are more guilt ridden.

They never look you in the eye. Most of them are bent over, hiding their faces, staring at the cracks in the sidewalk. They inhale and exhale, hoping not to be noticed by the passing crowd.

Father Crowly, of Our Lady of the Virginia Slims, ministers to those who are obsessed with the tobacco weed. He offered to give me a tour.

"This is my flock," he said, pointing to a group huddled in the doorway of the General Motors Building.

"They are so hopeless that no one else will have anything to do with them."

"They seem to be coughing a lot," I told him.

"That does not mean they are not good people. You see the fellow in the pin-striped suit with the Countess Mara necktie? He works for an advertising agency, and he's out on the sidewalk every seven minutes."

"What's so wrong with that?"

"He works on the fiftieth floor. Every time he sneaks down, he gets short of breath.

"The woman with her back to us is Regina Dumbarton. She is a two-pack-a-day person and is terribly frightened that if Clinton puts a new tax on cigarettes she will have to sell her apartment to pay for her habit. She could never afford those costs on the salary she makes at her health insurance firm."

"Father, is smoking a sin?"

"It will be if they put a new tax on it."

"What do you tell people who live in dread that this could happen?"

"I tell them to get down on their knees and pray to the tobacco lobby."

"How did you get involved in saving these souls?"

"One time the Marlboro man was in the confessional, and he was smoking. I breathed in his secondary smoke, and I was hooked."

"Then what?"

"The cardinal issued a decree that he didn't want smoking in church, so I went out on the sidewalk where I met all these addicts that no one cared for."

We walked past Saks Fifth Avenue. Customers as well as employees were standing outside the store, not speaking to one another but lighting their cigarettes as if they hoped to find a message there.

Father Crowly said, "Some of my hardest cases are customers who don't know if they should be inside or outside the store."

"What do you do for them?"

"Give them absolution as well as coffee and doughnuts. It can be darn cold in the winter smoking in the street. Most of these people have to have coffee with their cigarettes."

Father Crowly went up to one of the smokers standing in the shadow of Radio City Music Hall. The man's hand was shaking as he tried to light his smoke.

Father Crowly took out a Zippo and lit it for him.

"God bless you, Father," the man said.

Crowly tapped him on the head and replied, "Even chain-smokers need love."

Don't Sit Under That Apple Tree

SO IT'S FINALLY SETTLED. Gays can serve in the U.S. Armed Forces as long as they don't talk about it.

The Joint Chiefs of Staff call it an honorable compromise, and it sounds very easy to enforce.

And yet . . .

Somewhere in Somalia two Americans are in a foxhole. Pfc. Dumbarton says, "Austin, have you ever been in love?"

Austin Wilshire says, "Once, a few years ago. His name was Arnold."

"Wilshire, are you gay?"

"You're not permitted to ask me that, and I am not permitted to tell you. But Arnold was the only person I ever gave my heart to."

"Does the Army know that you loved Arnold?"

"I don't think so. If they did, I would be very upset since they aren't supposed to pry into my private life."

"What happened between you and Arnold?"

"He sent me a 'Dear John' letter."

"Why didn't he send you a 'Dear Austin' letter?"

"Because nobody sends a GI a 'Dear Austin' letter. When you kiss someone off, the letter has to come to John."

"My girl's name is Rhoda."

"Are you in love with a woman?"

"That's none of your damn business. The Army says that my sexual orientation is not a public matter. If I want to attend heterosexual movies with Rhoda and hang out in bars patronized equally by men and women—it's my privilege."

"Don't get upset. I'm not going to turn you in just because I heard about you dancing with a girl. At the same time, I don't expect you to report me because you see me sitting on a park bench with some Tom, Dick or Harry."

"I believe it's a terrible thing for a guy to break up with a soldier when the GI is overseas fighting for his country."

"I feel the same way. I never want to see Arnold again."

Dumbarton says, "It's lonely in Somalia. It's not one of those places where a guy can pick up a girl."

"Or a boy. The Army wants us to stay away from the locals because it would only complicate our mission."

"I can understand their thinking. I don't want to meet someone here and then be hurt when I have to leave."

"You mean a guy?"

"I don't have to tell you what I mean."

"Don't get mad at me. I was just curious about what kind of person you were going to leave behind."

"He could be bisexual, for all I know. There are no rules about falling in love with a bisexual."

"Of course not, unless you both walk down lovers' lane in drag. Would you like to see a picture of Rhoda?"

"I'd love to. Would you like to see a photo of Arnold?"

"Yes, very much. . . . He's handsome. I can see why the 'Dear John' letter upset you. He's worth fighting for.

"Like Kipling said, 'The civilians don't give a damn for you once the fighting stops.'"

Where the Money Is

I WISH TO MAKE ONE THING PERFECTLY CLEAR. The people of Martha's Vineyard have no intention of profiting from President Clinton and his wife, Hillary. We expect to make our money on the Secret Service. There are now an estimated fifteen thousand Secret Servicemen on the island, not counting Clint Eastwood, and they all eat pizza after every shift. So in every kitchen on the island, families are working twenty-four hours a day producing pizza for the president's bodyguards.

The first inkling we had that the president was coming here for his vacation was when two well-dressed gentlemen showed up in the chief of police's office in July. They told him, "We want two thousand of your people to guard the road, three thousand more on the beaches, and we'll take all the mounted patrolmen you've got."

The chief said, "I have only seven men on the force."

"Good," said the Secret Service agent. "We'll take them."

"Who is going to pay for it?" the chief asked.

"Don't worry. It will be in the president's next budget."

The vacationers and residents of Martha's Vineyard are torn as to whether they want the president on the island. In a recent referendum the resort was split 50 percent for and 50 percent against.

The vote was so close that the president is bringing in Vice President Al Gore to break the tie.

People are not faulting Mr. Clinton for coming here—it's that we islanders will never be the same after his visit.

Rumor has it that six luxury cruise ships jammed with tourists on their way to Bermuda heard the president was here, and the boats were ordered by the owners to turn around and head back at full steam for the Vineyard.

The ferries from the mainland are chock-full of day visitors who were all promised that if they bought tour tickets they could have a golf game with the president.

The restaurants are packed with hungry visitors who can't get anything to eat because all the college kids who have been working on the island have quit to "see" the president.

But the worst thing is the psychic blow inflicted on the people of the Vineyard. Everyone hopes in his heart to be invited to a social event attended by the president and Mrs. Clinton.

It's a typical have-and-have-not situation. Those who have invitations don't give a damn about those who don't. The people not invited have two choices: One is to say they wouldn't be caught dead at the Summer White House; the second is to put on their snorkel masks and refuse to talk about what they did while the Clintons were here.

Another way to handle not being invited is to pretend that you have been. It's no problem to fake it.

Did I see the Clintons when they were here? You know and I know I can't answer that question. Let's just say they drove us home after Jackie's dinner and leave it at that.

What I admire about the president when he's at the beach is that even if you make over $200,000 a year, he never kicks sand in your face.

What Honor Code?

THE NEWS FROM CAMBRIDGE, Massachusetts, is that 83 percent of all the undergraduates at MIT cheated at least once in their college careers. More than two-thirds confessed to plagiarism, and half admitted stealing other people's ideas.

What puzzled me about the survey was not that 83 percent cheated, but that 17 percent didn't.

I went to the campus to talk to the noncheaters.

They were huddled off in a corner, and none of the cheaters would have anything to do with them.

"How come you didn't cheat while you were in school?" I asked.

David Moskowitz replied, "No one taught us how."

Jane Mitchell said, "You learn cheating from your parents. I came from a happy home, and there was nobody around who knew how to beat the system."

Fred Calabash said, "I once asked my father if winning was everything. He replied, 'No, it isn't.' I figured that he didn't know what he was talking about, so I ran away."

"It seems to me that you're blaming your parents for not cheating. Can't you put some of the responsibility on yourselves? Let's say your folks refused to teach you how to lie, cheat and steal. Why didn't you go to your friends?"

Zelda Claghorn said, "That's easy for you to say. But I was afraid of getting caught."

"What's to be afraid of? Everyone in the country cheats. Defense contractors cheat, congressmen cheat, bankers cheat, the White House cheats and people driving leased automobiles cheat. The purpose of college is to teach you that cheating is a way of life in the United States. You people better start doing it right away if you hope to survive in a capitalist society."

David Moskowitz was adamant. "I've never plagiarized anything in my life."

"It's not too late to start now," I yelled at him.

"What about the honor code?" Carisa Clark asked.

"It's a good thing as long as no one is found out. But if you're brought up on charges, it breaks up fraternity houses."

Harry Redfern said, "I know some people who were honest and still finished school."

"And I know people who walked on the moon. The question is, how many?"

"Do you think that cheaters should be punished?" Margot Wild asked.

"I'm not sure," I replied. "I asked the dean if cheating is the worst thing that a student could do, and she replied, 'No. Attempting to park in the faculty parking lot without a sticker is a lot worse.'"

"Cheating is rampant on all campuses," Erik Miller said. "MIT is just the tip of the iceberg."

"MIT is a good school," I assured him. "Your exams are very difficult. You have to do everything you can to pass."

"Do you think that they'll kick us out of school for not cheating?" one of the students asked me.

"They'll probably give you a warning first. If you continue not cheating, they will be forced to take action."

Carson Blandford said, "I wish I had my academic life to live over again."

"Why?" I wanted to know.

"I'd put all my math test answers on my French cuffs."

Steady As She Goes

THE WORDS THAT SEEM TO BE POPPING UP all over Washington are "damage control." When discussing Clinton's difficulties with his investment in Whitewater, it is generally agreed that the problem is not the issue itself. The damage control is what's causing all the trouble.

Every president has highly trained damage-control teams that are expected to minimize any situation that could embarrass him.

As on a ship, the damage-control team is located below deck—in the boiler room of the White House. They are in touch with the top officers on deck who are steering the boat through the treacherous rocks of the scandal. When the alarm goes off, the damage-control team, wearing masks and oxygen tanks, does a survey to find out how bad things are.

Harris Block, a senior damage-control officer, calls up to the bridge, "There is a small leak in the boiler, and there are Whitewater papers floating all around."

"Can you plug it?" the executive officer asks from topside.

"It's too late. The leak is spreading," Block tells him.

"What do you advise?"

"We could bring down some divers from the Justice Department to gather what there is and get it off the ship."

"Good idea. And then deep-six the files."

But the damage-control leader says, "Too many people know about the files, and if they are dumped it might appear that we are covering up and that could lead to a court-martial."

A White House official shouts, "Media ship off the port side. They request permission to board and question the captain on why the ship of state is in such treacherous waters."

Block says, "Don't let them come on board. Send over six damage-control officers to deny what happened."

"Aye, aye, sir. Attention, media ship. All questions regarding damage to our vessel must be relayed to the Justice Department. They're the only ones who understand why we're taking on so much water."

A radio man speaks to the executive officer: "Sir, they want to appoint a special prosecutor to examine all the papers involved with the accident and to recommend court-martial charges against those who may be responsible for Whitewater."

The officer responds, "That's out of the question. Send back word that we can investigate our own accidents. Our damage-control people are the best in the business."

"That may not fly, sir. We should come up with something else."

"Tell them we're willing to cooperate in any way possible, but they can't board the ship until next Tuesday."

"Why next Tuesday?"

"So that we can get the ship all cleaned up and not have any bilge hanging around."

"Steady as she goes."

"Hard right rudder."

The executive officer turns to the helmsman and says, "Remind me to send our damage-control team a 'well-done.'"

Adolph the Great

THERE ARE ARGUMENTS IN FAVOR OF GUNS and arguments against them. Zoltan, a millionaire Hollywood producer, is the proud owner of a .45 semi Snout and showed it to me when we were driving to the racetrack in his Rolls-Royce.

"I keep Adolph right here on my lap," he confided. "If anybody gives me trouble, I go POW."

"That's terrific," I told him. "But isn't it tough to hold the gun in one hand and drive with the other?"

"Only if I have to make a phone call. I can't tell you what it means to hold a gun close to me when I am in the car. There are still a lot of crazy people driving on the California freeways, and most of them hate people in Rolls-Royces. But nobody fools with me. Adolph could wipe out a Greyhound bus if I wanted it to."

"Do you ever get the urge to shoot a person even if he didn't do anything?"

"Sure, I get the urge. If someone gets too close to me or cuts me off, he could find himself in Flanders Field alongside the poppies."

"I assume that nobody has made a move on you since you got the gun."

"No, but I wish they would. I wish the heck they'd honk at me just once. Adolph would like nothing more than to make them get on their knees and beg for mercy."

"Aren't you afraid that you might accidentally shoot yourself in the groin?"

"Not me. I was personally given safety instructions by Charlton Heston. I have also completed ten hours on the shooting range. People like me never shoot themselves in the groin."

Suddenly Zoltan whispered to me, "While we've been driving I've noticed three cars that could possibly ram my Rolls-Royce and total it. I have a good mind to fire a warning shot over their hoods."

I said, "I don't see them."

"Over there—the Pontiac with the two guys wearing baseball caps who are pointing at me, then the guy who's always checking his rearview mirror to keep his eye on me. Finally there's the car that passed by a half hour ago, and the driver laughed at me. My finger is getting itchy."

"Wait," I said. "If you make a mistake, they'll give you ten years. Maybe they're not even looking at the Rolls or, even if they are, it's only out of envy, not hostility."

Zoltan snorted. "You don't have any idea what it's like to own a Rolls. I drive to the shopping mart or to the car wash and someone follows me home and sticks me up in my driveway. Every time I go to the theater, someone is waiting to pounce. That's why I love Adolph. If those dirtbags come at me, he speaks for both of us."

"If everyone hates people in Rolls-Royces, why don't you drive a Honda?"

Zoltan almost went through the roof of his car. "With my money, who'd want to own a Honda?"

"Anybody who doesn't like to worry about being followed."

"It wouldn't be fair to trade in my Rolls for a Honda," Zoltan said. "What would I do with Adolph?"

I'm Glad You Asked

THERE SEEMS TO BE SOME CONFUSION about Whitewater, so let me answer some of your questions.

Q: What is Whitewater?

A: It's an underground river that runs through Arkansas, eastward, right into the White House Rose Garden.

Q: Is that all?

A: It is also a real estate investment. Some Arkansas hotshot developers tried to build retirement homes along the banks of the Whitewater and lost their shirts.

Q: What's wrong with that?

A: Nothing, except that nobody in the White House knows exactly how many shirts President Clinton and his wife lost.

Q: What's wrong with that?

A: The project was financed by the Madison Savings and Loan in Little Rock, and the bank went under with sixty million dollars' worth of the taxpayers' shirts.

Q: What's wrong with that?

A: No one seems clear about the relationship between the bank and the Clintons. They only know that Jim McDougal was a Good Friend of Bill.

Q: What business is that of anybody's?

A: None, except that every time the president discusses White-water he comes up with a different number for his losses, and that confuses the American people.

Q: Maybe he had a bad accountant.

A: That's a given. Whoever was keeping the books for the prez should be sent to a maximum-security boot camp for life.

Q: Did Mrs. Clinton's investment in the commodities market have anything to do with Whitewater?

A: Not unless she bought futures in frogs' legs. They say that she went into commodities hoping to recoup the money she had invested in Whitewater. Although the Clintons did not know too much about real estate, they became experts on soybeans when they were at Yale.

Q: Is the press being unfair by pursuing every investment the Clintons made?

A: Nobody is blaming the Clintons for their investments. But the media have a right to know where they found so many lousy accountants.

Q: What can the average American citizen do to show support for the president?

A: Buy one of the Whitewater lots. Almost all of them are still for sale. If it became another Levittown, the president would be vindicated for his business judgment in real estate and be hailed as another Donald Trump.

Q: All this happened years ago. Why is it suddenly coming up now?

A: Except for Bosnia, things are very quiet around the world, and Whitewater gives everyone a chance to read about something that doesn't affect them. Besides, Americans feel better knowing that even their president can't fill out a tax form correctly.

Q: Do you think that Hillary will play the commodities market again?

A: She'll probably try to stay out. Unfortunately, she's stuck with tons of goose livers, and she's going to have to unload them fast.

Q: Is Whitewater another Watergate?

A: No, but it isn't Sun Valley, either.

Expert Witness

ONE OF THE THINGS that makes the American legal system so fair is that in any civil suit lawyers are permitted to call "experts" who will testify in favor of their clients. There are now almost as many experts as lawyers in this country, and some of them make more money than the people they're working for.

I got the word on what an expert's profession is like by talking to Dr. Zeigfried Bibbleman in the hall of the Superior Court House of Los Angeles. He was waiting to be called to testify in a defective turf case.

"How long did you practice medicine before you became a legal expert?"

He replied, "I never actually practiced medicine. When I graduated from medical school I discovered that the really big money in doctoring was in the courtroom. I charge six hundred dollars an hour for testifying and seven hundred fifty for a second opinion. I have given testimony in almost two thousand lawsuits."

"On what basis do you choose your cases?"

"It depends on which lawyer gets to me first. In this case, I am here because the plaintiff got to me ahead of the defendant. I plan to testify that the plaintiff's injuries were caused by the faulty artificial turf when she slid into first base."

"But, Doctor, you can't sue when a person slides into first."

"So what? I'm the expert, and they'll have to take my word for it."

Dr. Bibbleman told me that hired medical experts are the key to successful malpractice suits. "Because we appear only in court-rooms and never in hospitals, we are the unsung heroes of our profession."

"Do you ever change your opinion about the cause of an injury during the course of the trial?"

"Once in a while."

"Was it because you felt that you were wrong?"

"No, it was because the lawyer was refusing to pay me. It was his mistake because the jury was flabbergasted when I switched horses in midstream."

"I assume that you testify for anyone?"

"I'll testify for the meter maid in the street if she can come up with the money. An expert doctor must serve one and all."

"What makes a good medical witness?" I asked.

"It's someone who swears to tell the truth, the whole truth, and nothing but the truth, and then spends the rest of his time on the stand lying through his teeth. But he has to look believable. That's why I always wear this stethoscope when I take the stand."

"How do lawyers know about you?"

"I have a reputation of being one of the most knowledgeable experts in the business and also for telling the court exactly what my client wants them to hear."

"What was your greatest triumph?"

"It was a dandruff case. The client was a shampoo company that was sued by a man who claimed that the product gave him dandruff instead of getting rid of it. I testified that the man had hay fever, and this in turn caused dandruff particles to attach themselves to his head when he sneezed."

"And the judge threw the man's case out?"

"Not only that, but because I had successfully testified in his court a hundred times, he invited me back for tea."

Law-Abiding What?

THE PHRASE THAT I HEARD the most during the debate on the Senate crime bill was "law-abiding citizens," as in "Will you deprive law-abiding citizens of their right to bear arms under the Second Amendment?" or "The law-abiding citizens of my state will not stand by if you take their semiautomatic weapons away from them."

I can't speak for others, but I don't know any law-abiding citizens. That doesn't mean they don't exist—it's just that I have never met them.

Take Rubbishon, who owns a Rapid Death .45 semiautomatic pistol. He broke all the environmental laws when he constructed his house and boasts about cheating on his income tax.

Charlie Tender is no better. He sports a sawed-off Jezebel Glockmeister and has an autographed photo of Charlton Heston on his wall. Charlie would be a law-abiding citizen except for the fact that he refuses to separate his bottles from the rest of his garbage.

Instead, he pays the refuse people $20 so they will look the other way. He also owns a bottling factory that is one of the biggest polluters in America.

Petty crimes, you might say, but as Arnold Schwarzenegger said in *Les Misérables,* "The law is the law."

Senators who believe that their constituents who keep firearms in their homes are protecting their private property are living in a dreamworld.

Most of the people killed at home are victims of a law-abiding loved one (or former loved one) who keeps a weapon in the house.

Professor Joe Skalet, who has been unsuccessfully searching for a law-abiding citizen ever since he graduated from Stanford, told me, "If there are any law-abiding citizens who own guns, they are very careless about where they keep them. Some time ago a man in No Drink, Michigan, hid his semiautomatic under the floor, sealed it with cement and then put a refrigerator over it.

"In just two days his eight-year-old son found it by moving the refrigerator, borrowing a jackhammer and digging up the floor. The boy took the gun to school and sprayed the entire fifth-grade gym class with gunfire."

John Dillinger once said, "There is no way a law-abiding citizen can hide a gun from an eight-year-old child."

Professor Skalet's studies indicate that law-abiding citizens go through as many red lights and exceed the speed limit twice as much as non-law-abiding members of society. They also brag a great deal about breaking the law, except, of course, where their guns are concerned.

In many cases, although they will fight to the death to preserve the Second Amendment, which provides them with the right to bear arms, they keep asking for the First Amendment to be thrown out of court on a technicality.

I mention all this only because I'm sick and tired of senators referring to their constituents as "law-abiding citizens" when they themselves break more laws than the rest of us.

What They Don't Tell You

HERE'S WHAT THEY DON'T TELL YOU about health-care costs. Every day someone invents a machine to save people's lives. Once it comes onto the market, doctors are obligated to use it. If they don't, some nasty lawyer will accuse them of malpractice. So the more the invention is used, the higher the cost of medical care.

For example, let's look at the Dingerscope, a new nuclear camera that permits the physician to examine every part of the human body from a crouching position.

This allows medical personnel to tell whether a patient is lying on his stomach or his back. Once the machine has established this, doctors are able to use the fifty other machines at their disposal to treat patients.

The cost of using the Dingerscope is $14,000, which does not include a 15 percent tip for the technician.

Here's an example of what we're talking about:

Stephanie Stefanini is brought into the hospital for possible acid indigestion. The doctor is prepared to prescribe medicine costing $1.50 when Kristi Fischer, one of the residents, tells him that the Dingerscope has arrived. She suggests that they use it to establish if there is any gas associated with the stomachache or not.

"That's a good idea," the doctor says. "How long will it take to prepare the patient for the machine?"

"Two days," the resident tells him. "It's just a question of availability. There is quite a line ahead of us, as this is a new machine and everyone has fallen in love with it."

"How much will it be?" Stephanie asks.

The doctor responds, "Please be quiet. You'll only aggravate your indigestion when you find out how much it costs."

Then the doctor turns to the resident and says, "Dr. Chris Spurney is in charge of the Dingerscope. Call him and ask him when we can come down."

"Dr. Spurney is playing golf because it's Wednesday. Dr. Jon Swerdloff is doing the Ding today, but there is a surcharge because the insurance company says that he's not qualified."

Meanwhile, Stephanie is becoming more and more uncomfortable and begs for fast relief.

The doctor instructs the nurse to hold her down.

"Mrs. Stefanini, my job as a physician is to use every piece of equipment in this hospital. Before the Ding appeared, you would have been out of here in twenty minutes. But since we have the machine, it would be a betrayal of my Hippocratic oath if I didn't put you under it."

"I appreciate that, Doctor, but one Ding procedure and I will have blown my entire health insurance allowance for the next six years. Is there any occasion where a doctor can treat a patient without sending him down to the nuclear smasher department?"

The doctor replies, "I have been practicing medicine for thirty years, and I have never known the hospital to buy a machine it does not use day and night."

The resident announced that the Ding was ready, and Stephanie was wheeled down into the lead-lined basement.

Her head was inserted into an opening, her shoulders were strapped to a trolley and her legs were placed around the soft-drink machine.

A technician entered the room and rubbed some ointment on Stephanie's stomach. Then he signaled his assistant to pull the lever. Out of the side of the machine came a piece of microfilm and a stick of bubble gum. The doctor read it and then handed Stephanie an Alka-Seltzer. The final bill was $25,000.

The Rumor Handlers

IT IS NO SURPRISE that election races have turned uglier and uglier. People don't realize that it's not the candidates who are mean and rotten—it's their handlers. Whenever a really disgusting rumor is spread, a candidate will disclaim any knowledge of it and blame it on some "misguided staff member who has been reprimanded."

As far as handlers are concerned, winning is everything, and they couldn't care less what political high crimes and misdemeanors they are charged with.

I saw proof of the technique when I visited the office of Charles Peanut who was running for the Senate against the incumbent, Will Willowbright.

A handler, wearing a bulletproof vest, came into the office to screen some videotape commercials.

The first showed a stripteaser doing her number.

The voice-over said, "Senator Willowbright doesn't know this woman, but he would like to. Protect your family—vote for Peanut."

"What do you think?" Peanut asked me.

"It does have a political message," I said.

The handler kept going. The next commercial showed Willowbright eating dinner at a large political fund-raiser. "While our boys were in Haiti, Senator Willowbright was eating swordfish at the Hilton Hotel. Now you know why Saddam Hussein misread American intentions in the Middle East."

I pointed out that it wasn't negative enough. "Not many Americans know who Saddam Hussein is or why we were in Haiti."

Peanut agreed. "Scrub it."

The handler pushed the tape button. The commercial showed a montage of criminals in prison, in handcuffs and chains. It ended with a close-up of the electric chair. "The reason you don't see Willowbright in this picture," the voice-over said, "is that he doesn't give a damn about crime." Then they have a shot of the country club. "The only thing he cares about is his golf game. Are your wives and daughters safer on the street because Willowbright can shoot an eighty-five?"

Peanut said, "I like it. I shoot an eighty-one, but I don't want us to sound as if we're running a negative campaign."

The handler turned to me. "We're working on some more—one showing Willowbright in and out of what we claim to be a crack house. It's actually a halfway house, but who's to know? We're also planning a shot of Willowbright with President and Mrs. Clinton."

"How did you get that?" Peanut asked.

"We took it with a camera hidden in Pat Buchanan's cigarette lighter. This year no campaign actually has a photo of a Democratic candidate with the president of the United States, and no candidate has admitted to ever having met Bill Clinton."

"So far so good. What else are we going to do with Willowbright?"

"We're calling him a liar."

"What for?"

"It doesn't matter. He has to prove that he isn't."

"Suppose he charges us with hitting him below the belt?"

"We'll tell him to lower his belt."

"You're a good man, Dirk Dagger. If I am elected, I'll see to it that you become director of the Political Ethics Committee."

"Politics is a pure and honorable profession—but someone has to do it."

Bell on the Telephone

IT HAS BEEN CONFIRMED that Alexander Graham Bell is turning over in his grave. His simple invention, which he called the telephone (for want of a better name), has become a joke, and he finds nothing funny about it.

Had Bell been inventing today with his dear friend Watson, here's what might have happened:

Watson and Bell have been working day and night trying to perfect the telephone. Finally, Bell goes into another room, spills acid in his lap and says painfully into the phone, "Watson, come here, I wish to talk to you."

Instead of Watson hearing it, a voice comes on and says, "If you know the name of your doctor and you are at a touch-tone phone, press one. If you don't know the name of your party but would like to date his sister, press two. If you wish to take a trip to Alaska, press three. If this is an emergency, please enter your Social Security number, your Blue Cross registration card number and spell out the names of two people who will vouch for you, then press four. If you would like to speak to Dr. Watson, please stay on the line while Mstislav Rostropovich conducts the National Symphony Orchestra in the complete works of Beethoven."

Much to his horror, Bell realizes that, instead of inventing the phone, he has invented voice mail. This, of course, is not what he had in mind. In his original papers Bell wrote, "It is my fervent wish that this telephone invention will be an instrument whereby people can talk to each other without interference from a tape recording."

Bell went on to write, "I have no idea what man will do with this wonderful instrument and whether it will be used for good or evil. I am aware that there are a lot of sleazy salesmen out there who can persuade stupid business executives, educated at Harvard, that it is in their interests to have a tape recording instead of a person answer the phone. The argument will be that a tape machine can save the salaries of two telephone operators. I pray to heaven that this doesn't happen because when a live voice is replaced by a recording something inside of a telephone dies."

Bell also foresaw that once the government broke up his phone company, which it considered a monopoly, a group of Baby Bells would be created. These companies would be more concerned with cable television and other profit-making businesses than with the phone.

In a letter to his friend Thomas Michael Keyes, he said, "I know that I cannot control what my invention will be used for, but I have a foreboding that Wall Street will corrupt it by urging phone companies to go into movie production and baseball franchises. I predict that people will try to profit from all that I've done by having nine hundred numbers where you can talk dirty to someone by pressing one.

"I urge you, Thomas, that if this happens you will yank out the phones of all who have them and take my name off all the companies that use it."

What made Alexander Graham Bell a genius was that he envisioned the perversion of his invention. In his diary he wrote that the phone company would break even on calls and coin most of its money on repairmen coming to subscribers' homes to fix the phones. He also saw the phone companies making a bonanza from the wrong numbers that people would dial without their glasses.

The final words Bell wrote to Watson were "I tried to call you on the phone and tell you about the acid in my lap, but I forgot to press one."

The Road to Ruin

THE CAPITAL BELTWAY IS NOT ONLY a highway to accommodate bumper-to-bumper traffic; it has also become a metaphor for what is wrong with the country.

Every politician running for office blames our troubles on the people "inside the Beltway." Almost everyone who wins a national election campaigned against the Washington insiders who have no idea what "real" Americans want.

But then the day of reckoning arrives. The elected who have come to Washington must sit inside the Beltway and write the laws of the nation.

I was driving along near Exit 33 when I came across an incredible scene. Two federal marshals were trying to shove a handcuffed man into an unmarked sedan.

"What's up, officers?" I inquired.

One of the marshals said, "This is a newly elected congressman, and he refuses to go inside the Beltway."

The congressman was blubbering. "Please don't make me go in there. They'll eat me alive. I'll burn in Hell. They'll plunge daggers in my back." He tried to run, but the marshals held him tight.

"It's not that bad," I told him. "Some people live very comfortably inside the Beltway. We have electricity and telephones and even indoor plumbing."

The man was completely distraught. "I campaigned against those inside the Beltway—the bureaucrats and the big spenders who don't give a hoot about the little man. If I go in there now, they'll tar and feather me."

"People inside the Beltway don't hold grudges, except against the Washington Redskins. I doubt if anyone remembers what you said about us during your election campaign."

He tried to escape again. "I'm going home to be with normal folks, and I'll vote from there," the man said.

"You can't do that. The Constitution states clearly that a congressman must cast his ballot inside the Beltway for any legislation to become the law of the land. I've seen people like you come to this town afraid of their own shadow and in less than six months they're driving around Washington as if they owned it."

The congressman said, "If I go inside, will I be blamed for the deficit?"

"Of course not. Hillary Clinton is solely responsible for that, and Chelsea is to blame for all the money being wasted on our military cost overruns. If your middle-class constituents won't buy that, you can always offer them a tax cut."

The federal marshal said, "Come on, sir. They're waiting for you to make a quorum."

The congressman got into the vehicle reluctantly.

"If I'm going to take my seat in Congress, I want an air bag to go with it."

Meals with Wheels

THE DEMOCRATS HAVE PUT a "For Sale" sign on the White House. It was announced that if you give $100,000 to the party, you are entitled to: two meals with the president; attend two events with Vice President Gore; a spot on a foreign trade commission with party and business leaders; several impromptu meetings with various administration officials; plus a daily fax report (I did not make any of this up).

For $50,000 you can go to a presidential reception, have dinner with Al Gore and attend special policy briefings.

Ten thousand dollars brings you a presidential reception and orchestra seats at the Democratic National Convention.

The big bargain is, in exchange for $1,000, the donor receives an invitation to meet Hillary Rodham Clinton, Tipper Gore and female political appointees.

While all these incentives sound perfectly legal to me, there have to be some political observers who are worried that the donor program could get out of hand.

I know a very rich man, Joe Glover, who told me he had just written out his check and was sending it over to the White House by messenger.

"I have a few things I want to tell the president, and I really need him to pay attention."

"What makes you think that he will listen?" I asked Joe.   •

"Because money talks. I have no problem putting the White House on my payroll, and if they want to throw in Al Gore as my dinner partner, so be it."

"Maybe the Democratic National Committee is just pulling your leg, and after they cash your check, they will seat you 'below the salt'—way down at the end of the dining table—next to George Stephanopoulos."

Glover said, "No way. I have been promised a seat on Clinton's right at breakfast or across from him at dinner, whichever comes first. I also have been asked to serve on a foreign trade mission. For an additional fifty thousand dollars I get to set the federal interest rates for September. When it comes fund-raising, the White House knows how to treat its donors.

"I even heard there's talk that for a million dollars contributors are entitled to a choice of meeting with Arafat or Peres and negotiating a Middle East peace treaty, or inspecting a nuclear facility in North Korea. I find that pretty exciting."

"And well you should. How does your wife feel about meeting with Hillary Clinton and Tipper Gore?"

"Everyone in Glen Oaks is green with envy. It's considered one of the best buys of the summer."

Joe believes it is an American's duty not only to participate in government but also to pay for it. He also thinks that by buying in at this time a person can be helpful to the administration, as it gives the president an opportunity to talk to the grassroots people for a bargain price.

Glover explained, "I want to get in on the ground floor because I think the day will come when the price of a meal with the president could go soaring into seven figures, and only the really fat cats will be able to afford it. Right now being able to eat scrambled eggs with the president for a hundred thousand dollars is something any member of the middle class can afford."

Smokers' Lucky Strike

THE FLORIDA ATTORNEY GENERAL'S decision to sue the tobacco companies could be a big bonanza for lawyers.

Everyone who ever smoked a cigarette will be joining the class-action suit.

I was in Palm Beach the other day when I overheard the conversation of two people standing outside Saks Fifth Avenue.

The man lit up two cigarettes and then handed one to his companion.

"Who is your lawyer?" he asked the woman.

She inhaled deeply and replied, "Arnold and Porter. I tried to get Mayer, Brown and Platt, but they had a conflict because they were representing the tobacco auctioneers of America. Who's yours?"

The man puffed nervously. "Kaye, Scholer. I showed them an X ray of my chest and they said they'd take me on contingency, although I do have to pay expenses."

"Are you going to go for a jury trial?" the woman asked.

The man said, "My lawyer feels it's the only way to go, providing we can get twelve jurors who are nonsmokers."

"I have a friend who sued Philip Morris and had F. Lee Bailey as counsel. He won ten million, but the judge threw it out."

"How come?" the man asked.

"Apparently one of the jurors had sold his horse to the Marlboro Man. Have we got time for one more?"

They lit up two more cigarettes. "I'm requesting compensation for pain and suffering. People treat you like a leper if you start puffing on a cigarette in their presence."

The woman agreed. "You can say that again. Half the eligible men in this town won't go out with me because I smoke."

The man started to blow smoke rings in the air.

"It's gotten so bad that every time I light a cigarette after making love to my wife, she makes me go outside."

The woman said, "That's awful."

"It's worse than that. Our apartment is on the thirty-fourth floor."

The woman asked, "Do you suppose they'll let us smoke in the courtroom?"

The man replied, "My lawyer told me that even if they did he didn't think it would make a good impression on the jury."

Suite Revenge

LEOLA STARLING, OF RIBROCK, TENNESSEE, had a serious telephone problem. But, unlike most people, she did something about it.

The brand-new $10 million Ribrock Plaza Motel opened nearby and had acquired almost the same telephone number as Leola.

From the moment the motel opened, Leola was besieged by calls—not for her. Since she had had the same phone number for years, she felt she had a case to persuade the motel management to change its number.

Naturally, the management refused—claiming it could not change its stationery.

The phone company was not helpful, either. A number was a number, and just because a customer was getting someone else's calls twenty-four hours a day didn't make it responsible. After her pleas fell on deaf ears, Leola decided to take matters into her own hands.

At nine o'clock the phone rang. Someone from Memphis was calling the motel and asked for a room for the following Tuesday. Leola said, "No problem. How many nights?"

A few hours later Dallas checked in. A secretary wanted a suite with two bedrooms for a week.

Emboldened, Leola said the Presidential Suite on the tenth floor was available for $600 a night. The secretary said she would take it and asked if the motel wanted a deposit.

"No, that won't be necessary," Leola said. "We trust you."

The next day was a busy one for Leola. In the morning she booked an electric appliance manufacturers' convention for Memorial Day weekend, a college prom and a reunion of the 82nd Airborne veterans from World War II.

She turned on her answering machine during lunchtime so she could watch the soaps, but her biggest challenge came in the afternoon when a mother called to book the ballroom for her daughter's wedding in June.

Leola assured the woman that it would be no problem and asked if she would be providing the flowers or whether she wanted the motel to take care of it. The mother said she would prefer that the motel handle the floral arrangements. Then the question of valet parking came up. Once again, Leola was helpful. "There's no charge for valet parking, but we always recommend that the client tip the drivers."

In a few months the Ribrock was a disaster area.

People kept showing up for weddings, bar mitzvahs and Sweet Sixteen parties and were all told there were no such events.

Leola had her final revenge when she read in the local newspaper that the motel might go bankrupt. Her phone rang, and an executive from Marriott said, "We're prepared to offer you two hundred thousand dollars for the motel."

Leola replied, "We'll take it, but only if you change the telephone number."

Part Three

The Quick and the Dead

EVERYONE IS TALKING ABOUT MEDICARE and the costs of health care. Intent on cutting costs, health insurance companies are now dictating the amount of time a patient can stay in the hospital. There is tremendous pressure on hospitals to toss patients out as fast as possible.

Thus the demands of the insurance industry are forcing new methods on everyone in dealing with the sick.

I paid a visit to Our Lady of Beth David in Doubledoon, Maryland, and it was an eye-opening experience.

Nancy Webking, the hospital director, told me, "We have no choice. If we don't get rid of our patients by their insurance deadlines, we're stuck with their bills."

"How do you get them out on time?"

"Through innovations. For example, we can now discharge someone who has had a triple bypass operation in one hour and three minutes."

"That's miraculous," I said.

Nancy explained, "We built a chute from the operating room, and as soon as the surgery is completed we slide the patient straight down into the parking lot."

"Doesn't the patient have any time in the recovery room?"

"Not unless his insurance policy specifies it."

"That must really hurt you to have to discharge a patient so soon."

"We don't enjoy it, but we have no say anymore as to who stays in the hospital and who goes."

"Suppose a patient is really sick with a high fever and can't eat any food. Would you still discharge him?"

"We'd call his health insurance company and let it make the decision. It employs high school tenth-graders part-time to man its phones. They are the ones who have the final say on major medical decisions."

"Do you ever get lucky and admit a patient whose policy entitles him to stay in the hospital for more than forty-eight hours?"

Nancy sighed. "No, but we had a patient once who couldn't pass a kidney stone. He was in so much pain that he said he would pay for the room out of his own pocket. So he stayed for two days and became like one of the family. He was such a nice man that we didn't charge him for his hospital robe."

"What has happened to your staff because of the austerity? Have you cut back on nurses?"

"We can't, because you never know when we'll get a patient who is covered by both Medicare and Blue Cross—and is entitled to stay in the hospital a full week."

Daddy Dumbest

I LOVE FATHER'S DAY. It's not just the gifts, or the choice of pie or strawberry shortcake that is offered to me, but I love the way my children treat me like the village idiot.

There comes a time in every father's life when the father-child role is reversed, and the offspring give the orders, and the patriarch accepts it because he has no choice. I can't pinpoint the exact moment when I began to be patronized, but once you go down that road there is no turning back.

I first noticed that things weren't the same when my children started to talk about me at the dinner table as if I weren't there.

"He looks very good," one child remarked, "although I wish he would exercise more."

My son said, "I tried to get him out on the tennis court the other day, but he said that he'd rather watch a golf tournament on TV."

My oldest daughter asked, "Do you think he wants any more mashed potatoes?"

Instead of protesting this treatment, I just nodded my head and grinned like Forrest Gump whenever they looked in my direction. Every once in a while one of the children would give me a thumbs-up.

I also noticed that they had started to speak to me more slowly and much louder than they did to one another.

"D-i-d y-o-u have a g-o-o-d week, Dad?"

I nodded, although I sensed that they really didn't care if I did or not. They just wanted to find a way to include me in the conversation.

I almost said that I got an A in history or something. Instead, I played with my string beans.

After dinner the serious whispering started. "He really is looking very healthy," my daughter told her brother.

My other daughter added, "He may look all right, but don't ask him to do any push-ups."

My son said, "Nobody would believe he fought in World War Two."

My daughter laughed. "I hope he doesn't start telling us how he single-handedly beat the Japanese again."

My son sounded sympathetic. "It's better to let him reminisce than to try and shut him up."

I am not complaining about the role my children have assigned to me. It is a normal progression in what is known in life as "passages."

Besides, being patriarch of the family took a lot out of me. My being treated as the village idiot is much more relaxing and gives tremendous pleasure to the other members of the family.

From Here to Infiniti

BECAUSE I PLAYED A PIVOTAL ROLE in World War II and was the only person who told President Roosevelt not to invite the Japanese ambassador to the White House for Christmas carols, I am very nervous about the recent snarling between our two countries.

We became involved in World War II over trade problems with Japan. I am therefore anxious that this should not happen again, especially during the year when we are celebrating the fiftieth anniversary of the end of the Good War. For this reason I call Pearl Harbor by phone every Sunday morning.

"Is anything going on?" I usually ask a Navy lieutenant.

"Nothing unusual, sir. It's very peaceful, and the officers are still asleep."

"Get them up!" I shout. "Right now."

"I can't do that on a Sunday morning. They all went to the club dance last night, and they are very tired. Is something wrong, sir?"

"I have a hunch. Our government had been thinking of banning the import of all Lexus cars, and the rumor is that the Japanese will boycott McDonald's French fries. Look outside your window. Do you see any airplanes coming in from the west?"

"No, sir. It's an uneventful Sunday morning in Pearl Harbor, and if we thought otherwise we would have everyone on alert."

"Where are the naval vessels?"

"All lined up in the harbor, neat as a pin."

"Take them out of there right now."

"I can't do that. Half the crews are on leave, and if we pulled them out they wouldn't be able to find their way home."

"Where are the fighter planes?"

"Lined up on the runway—exactly two feet apart, just as the Pentagon manual requires."

"Spread the planes out in bunkers."

"I can't do that, sir. The Air Force likes to line up its planes methodically."

"Lieutenant, have you ever heard the expression 'Tora, Tora, Tora'?"

"Is that a car or a TV set?"

"It's a code word. That's what Japanese businessmen say to each other whenever they feel that they have lost on a big Toyota deal. The next thing you know, every salesman jumps into his bomber cockpit and flies to Pearl Harbor."

"Have no fear, sir. It couldn't happen here. We are constantly on alert. Last Sunday a bunch of Japanese tried to break through by dumping Honda washing machines on the base. Wait a minute. I think I can hear plane engines. Oh my word! There are a lot of them, and they have rising suns painted on the side. They're not supposed to be here."

"Then shoot them down."

"I can't, sir."

"Why not?"

"Most of the officers here drive Infinitis, and they're not going to fire on their only source of spare parts."

"Lieutenant, our very way of life is threatened by the trade negotiations. There is now talk that if we ever boycott them, the Japanese will close down all the movie studios they own in Hollywood, which would mean the end of movie violence as we know it. Get the troops out of bed and destroy anything that fires on you. You owe it to the Navy. Remember the Day of Infamy."

"I hate to tell you this, sir, but I don't even remember the Bay of Pigs."

The Pitch: Hype and Inside

THE NAME OF THE GAME, no matter what the sport, is how much testimonial money is in it for each player. With that in mind, I have rewritten "Casey at the Bat."

It looked extremely rocky for Madison Avenue that day,
The score was 2 to 4 with but one commercial left to play.
When Cooney went to Pepsi and Burrows went to Coke,
It seemed as if the Snapple account would all go up in smoke.
The Reebok crowd got up to go, leaving Nike in the stands,
With hopes that Dewey would hit a homer with his Nivea lotion
    hands.
Everyone said if only Casey could get a whack at the ball
He'd sell a lot of Fruit of the Loom at the JCPenney mall.
But Flynn preceded Casey, with a special laptop brand,
While Blake was in the locker room with a Lite Beer in his
    hand.
So on the stricken multitude a deathlike silence fell,
And when Casey appeared in Calvin Klein jeans, the fans let
    out a yell.

There was ease in Casey's manner as he stepped into his place.

He signed a deal to spit Skoal snuff from the middle of his face.

Ten thousand eyes were on him as he rubbed his bat with
Squirt,

Five thousand hands applauded as he waved his blue Guess?
shirt.

And now the Gucci-covered sphere came hurtling through
the air,

And Casey stood a-watching it as he sipped a Red Dog beer.

Close by the sturdy batsman the ball unheeded sped,

Casey sneered at the pitcher and told him to drop dead.

"That ain't my style," said Casey. "Strike," the umpire said.

Casey chewed up all his Wheaties and drank some Gallo wine.

There were still two strikes to go so he would slowly bide his
time.

The sneer is gone from Casey's lips, his teeth are clenched
with hate.

He just found out what Michael Jordan makes when he gets
up to home plate.

And now the pitcher holds the ball and now he lets it go.

And now the air is shattered by the force of Casey's blow.

Oh, somewhere in this favored land the Nielsens shine so
bright.

The band is playing somewhere and the bread is very light.

Somewhere Pete Rose is laughing and somewhere Madden
shouts,

But there is no joy in Frito-Lay, mighty Casey just struck out.

Vacation Evacuation

THE CLINTONS AREN'T COMING to Martha's Vineyard, but the Danielses are. Helen and Everett Daniels are good friends of mine from Washington.

Everett called me in the spring to say that he wanted to rent a large house on the Vineyard.

"How large?" I asked.

"Large enough to accommodate everyone in the family—our five kids and their guests, who all say that they are dying to come."

I called an agent, and she found a lovely seven-bedroom place overlooking the ocean, which costs $5,000 a month. The price didn't bother Everett because, as he said, "You only go around Cape Cod once."

As soon as he signed the lease, Polly, the Danielses' sixteen-year-old, announced that she was going to a dude ranch in Colorado to be with her best friend. Steve, their eighteen-year-old, told his parents that he was going camping in Canada for the summer and not to count on him visiting the Vineyard for more than two days.

Lucy, who had a boyfriend named Terry, said, "Terry and I don't want to be around the family that much. We're going on vacation in Ocean City, where nobody will give us a hard time because we want to stay in the same room."

Everett saw the number of occupants of the Vineyard house dwindling fast. At dinner that evening he said, "I'm spending a lot of money on this place, and now only Cameron and Lila are coming."

"I'm not coming, Dad," Cameron announced. "I got a job running errands for a law firm, and it's a great opportunity for the time when I finish college."

"So now the only person left is Lila." Helen sighed.

Lila declared, "I want to go to camp."

"You told us that you didn't want to go to camp," Everett yelled.

"That was before I heard about Martha's Vineyard."

"Maybe we can get our money back," Helen said.

Everett was determined. "I'm going no matter what the rest of the family is planning. You and I will have a good time, Helen, and we'll finally get some peace and quiet."

Helen looked at him nervously.

"What is it? Say whatever's on your mind," said Everett.

"I was just wondering—if none of the children is coming, maybe it would be a good time to visit my mother in Scranton."

A Poke in the Nose

WHEN PRESIDENT CLINTON SAID he would like to punch columnist Bill Safire in the nose for calling Clinton's wife a "congenital liar," everyone in Washington stopped arguing about who had the highest snowbank in front of his house and instead discussed the fistic state of the White House.

Malcolm Mergenthaler, a presidential historian, said that the president's desire to sock a journalist came as no surprise.

He told me, "Every president, save George Washington, has wanted to punch a newspaperman in the nose. Some have even wanted to punch three or four, and we know of a few presidents who would have liked to punch a woman correspondent as well."

When the *New York Herald Tribune* slandered Jacqueline Kennedy, President Kennedy's first reaction was to punch the *Trib*'s White House writer in the nose. But his secretary of state thought it might further the career of the scribe and get him a raise. So, instead of a punch, the president canceled his subscription to the paper. That, on the surface, looked like a perfect compromise, but the president always regretted not taking more physical action. Arthur Schlesinger said the president told him the next time somebody wrote something he didn't like, he would not take the coward's way out. A few months later the president hit Khrushchev in the nose with such force that the Russian leader blinked.

The smart money in Washington says if the president and Safire resorted to fisticuffs, Clinton could take Safire in two rounds. President Clinton has a much longer reach and is in better shape than the columnist, who is known to have an exercise bicycle in his house that he never uses.

Also, if Safire landed even a weak left to the president's jaw, the Secret Service, by law, would have to mow the columnist down.

The subject has been discussed in the White House for days. Rather than cause the president any grief, the kitchen cabinet has voted to have Hillary Clinton punch Safire in the nose instead. She could catch Safire off guard, as he would be expecting the blow to come from the president.

The White House considers this an urgent matter because if something isn't done to sock Safire, no First Lady will ever be safe from name-calling again.

The Candidates Ad-Lib

HERE ARE THE POLITICAL COMMERCIALS you will never see on television.

"Hi, I'm Steve Forbes, and I paid for this commercial with my own money. I'm running for president because I am the only one who can afford it. I may not be the best man for the job, but when I get my flat tax, I'll be a lot more fun than the other candidates. If you don't understand my flat-tax proposal, I'll fly you to New Jersey and personally explain it to you."

"Call me Lamar Alexander. Steve Forbes has spent twenty million dollars on his campaign. This doesn't bother me because it's his money, and he has every right to allocate his funds to good clean commercials that educate all of us in the political process. The American people will regret not making him their candidate. As for myself, I am not against you voting for me the first time around as long as you don't make a habit of it."

"Hi, my name is Pat Buchanan, and like everyone else running for president, I'm praying that the best man wins and the Republican Party comes out on top. Maybe I don't have all the answers, my friends, but that doesn't mean I am not a good and honest man who has all his suits made in Mexico. No matter if I win or lose, I will fight to the death to allow every voter to carry a gun during the primaries. I have been criticized for having racists, white supremacists, and anti-Semites on my staff. Well, nobody is perfect. At least they're not illegal immigrants from El Salvador."

"Hi, I am Robert Dornan, and the difference between me and the other presidential candidates is that if I am elected I would be willing to nuke Havana to solve the Cuban problem once and for all. I am a cute guy, and what this country needs right now is a cute guy for president. I may not be as cute as Senator Alfonse D'Amato, but I'm cute enough to live in the White House."

"My name is Bob Dole, and as Senate majority leader everyone calls me 'Chuckles.' I am asking for your vote today, not because I am the most qualified person for the office, but because I am a veteran of World War Two. I have no better ideas for the country than Bill Clinton does, but I believe that we should have a seasoned man over seventy at the helm of this great nation. My Republican opponents have been taking a lot of cheap shots at me, but I know that they don't mean it. They're all good and dedicated men, and I am proud to run against them. If I am unsuccessful, I am not going to blame anybody but my own inept campaign. If you don't vote for me, why not take another look at Louis Farrakhan?"

The Upside of Downsizing

I HADN'T PLANNED TO WRITE ANYTHING about downsizing for a while until I read in the papers that Robert Allen, the CEO of AT&T, received $16 million in salary and stock option compensation. He was given $16 million at the time his company laid off 40,000 workers. When questioned about it, he said he deserved every penny.

One of my friends who doesn't understand downsizing was out-
raged. I tried to explain to him how it works.

"It takes a very talented executive to lay off forty thousand
employees, and sixteen million is not out of the ballpark if you
want someone to play hardball."

MacDougal asked, "What is Allen going to do with sixteen
million?"

I told him, "He has to buy milk and bread, and cornflakes and
yogurt, just like everybody else. You have to remember that sixteen million isn't what it used to be. What's important about the
layoffs is that Wall Street now views AT&T as a serious company.
The people who were pink-slipped don't count. If Wall Street sees
that the phone company is paying its chief sixteen million, they
have confidence in the management.

"They know that you don't hand paychecks like that to the big
guys unless the company has great plans for the future. Wall
Street is in the tea-leaf reading business, and they consider big
salaries for big people to be a good sign, even if middle management is asked to walk the plank."

MacDougal was not to be persuaded.

"I still don't understand what he can do with the whole sixteen
million. How many cordless phones can Allen have in his house?
How many cellular phones can he use in his Mercedes-Benz?
How many golf balls does a CEO need?"

I tried to be patient and replied, "Allen has to buy shoes for his
children, bus tokens for his wife, and he probably has a big heat-
ing bill. I very much doubt that any of the money will be spent on
luxuries."

MacDougal had the poor taste to bring up the 40,000 people
who had been laid off. "Don't you think they feel wounded to see

the man who dumped them receiving sixteen million for being their executioner?"

"When you downsize, you can't be sentimental about people. Allen claims he had to fire the forty thousand to save the company. If this is true, we Americans have to bless him for saving our long-distance lines."

"Do you trust him?" MacDougal asked.

"Maybe he was laying it on a bit thick, but he has to say something or the AT&T Credit Union would have refused to cash his sixteen million check."

MacDougal wasn't giving up. "Who decides how much a CEO is going to get for laying off thousands of people?"

"The board of directors."

"Who chooses the board of directors?"

"The CEO."

Every Pothole Has a Silver Lining

WASHINGTON HAS JUST HAD its worst winter in a century. The good news about this is that we are once again the pothole capital of the world, a title we lost to Buffalo in 1983.

What does it take to win the "Hole in One" cup?

Bad weather, rock salt and a "can-do" mayor.

Although the American people are always complaining about what goes on inside the Capital Beltway, we are still envied for our potholes. Many of them are so large that an aircraft can disappear into one and never be heard of again.

During the Cold War the Soviets always suspected our potholes were missile sites and accused us of violating the SALT agreement. After we permitted them to inspect our roads, they agreed that the only threat the potholes posed was to motorists in the District of Columbia.

When word was leaked that Washington had regained the "Hole in One" title, some taxpayers asked, "When the city is supposed to be practicing fiscal restraint, why is it constructing new potholes?" The answer to this is our potholes do not cost one cent. They are created free by heavy, out-of-town trucks, buses and automobiles.

The drivers donated their services. Some even dug the holes all night long in the freezing cold.

Our beloved mayor, Marion Barry, gets credit not only for ensuring that the city is well supplied with holes but also for insisting they be distributed all over town. By the way, there is no charge for hitting a pothole except what it costs to repair your vehicle. The mayor feels the holes are a good investment because they encourage tourism. Visitors from all over the country come here and then go back home to try to replicate the holes—which is impossible.

The custodian of Washington potholes, who makes sure they are never filled, is Timothy Maybank. He told me, "Our Founding Fathers were familiar with potholes and knew the country could not survive without them. They used the ones in Philadelphia as a model while drawing up plans for the streets in D.C. When the capital was moved here, horses and wagons from Wilmington, Delaware, were purposely imported to create the holes, and many from that period still exist. Some are even designated as national monuments."

To honor the occasion, each spring Washington holds a national Pothole Day when eighteen-wheelers from all over the United States descend on the city. There are prizes for the widest hole and the longest one, with a grand trophy for the "Pothole of the Year."

The day is sponsored by the vehicle-repair and body-shop industries, which offer to tow away, without charge, any conveyance that has had its underside damaged beyond repair.

There are other cities and towns—Queens, New York, comes to mind—that maintain they have even larger potholes than Washington. I have been to Queens, and I have ridden its rutted streets from La Guardia Airport to New York City. Its potholes are sand and pebbles compared with ours on Constitution Avenue.

As I write this, hundreds of vehicles are being swallowed by Washington roads. Are we upset over this? Hardly. Every morning we wake up and say, "Thank you, Mayor Barry. Just point our wheels in the right direction. We either sink or swim with you."

The Ace of Clubs

OF ALL THE ITEMS UP FOR SALE at the Jackie Kennedy Onassis auction, the one that impressed me the most was Lot 755: a set of golf clubs in a red-and-black bag with the initials "JFK" monogrammed on the outside. The item sold for $772,500, and the buyer was Arnold Schwarzenegger, an avid restaurant owner.

Since I don't play golf, I couldn't tell if Arnold got a bargain or not. So I called around to friends who are crazy about the sport.

The first person I called was David Wolper, a leading film producer. David didn't think that $772,500 was too much for a set of golf clubs. "For his money, Arnold got the clubs, the bag and at least a dozen golf balls. If you tried to purchase that at Kmart they would charge you double."

"Why didn't you buy them?" I asked him.

"It was just bad luck. At the time they were being auctioned, I was out playing golf."

I called George Stevens, a top amateur player on the circuit, who turned down an opportunity to become the U.S. ambassador to the Court of St. James because he heard that British golfers do not replace their divots.

George said, "I would have bought them myself, but Arnold is a good friend of mine, and I would do anything to save his game."

My next call was to Jack Valenti, who has devoted his life to golf, even if it has cost him many friendships and goodwill in Hollywood. Jack said, "Only someone who has shot a ninety-eight can appreciate a person paying seven hundred seventy-two thousand five hundred dollars to improve his swing. People just don't understand the importance of equipment in golf. There were two sets of golf clubs for sale. The other one went for three hundred and fifty thousand. I don't believe that any self-respecting golfer would play with the three-hundred-and-fifty-thousand set. As a matter of fact, with the cheaper clubs they wouldn't even let him on the course at Burning Tree."

Dean Smith, a money manager, was upset. "Arnold knew all along that I wanted those clubs, and he heard that I was willing to bid up to six hundred and ninety thousand for them. That's why he went to seven hundred seventy-two thousand five hundred. I'm waiting for Ivana Trump's garage sale, and when she offers to sell Donald Trump's putter, Arnold is going to be in serious trouble."

Sheldon Hackney was the only one who thought that Arnold had paid too much. "Personally, I have never paid more than five hundred thousand for a set of clubs, and if you keep your eye on the ball, you can save two hundred twenty-two thousand."

Except for Hackney, everyone I talked to envied Schwarzenegger and maintained that he had done the right thing. Don Brown, a real estate executive, said, "It's good for golf. The more money you pay for equipment, the more cachet the game acquires. At our house we had a 'Gift of the Magi' situation. My wife wanted to sell our BMW to purchase the JFK clubs for me, and I wanted to sell my humidor to buy her Jackie's simulated pearl necklace."

A Tankful of Liquid Capital

I DROVE TO THE GAS STATION the other day. The man asked, "How much gas do you want?" I looked at my bankbook and replied, "How about five gallons?"

The man said, "What do you plan to put up as collateral?"

"How about my car?" I asked.

"Everybody who comes in here wants to put up his car as collateral."

"But I need gas badly. This thing won't run without it."

"You should have thought of that when you bought it."

"Will you give me five gallons for this Rolex watch?"

"All my customers try to give me Rolex watches. For gas, I want cash."

"Why is the gas so expensive?" I wanted to know.

"Because the refineries can't produce enough to satisfy consumer demand."

"Why not?"

"Because if they satisfied the demand, the price of gas would go down again. Gasoline producers have to eat, too."

"Maybe I could afford three gallons if you make sure not to spill any when you put it in the tank."

"Okay, but I want the money in advance. Lots of people ask me to put the gas in the tank, and when they can't pay for it I have to siphon it out. It's tough on my lungs."

I handed him the key to my tank.

He inserted the nozzle. I watched as the needle slowly rose on the dashboard, and I heard the joyous sound of "gurgle, gurgle, gurgle."

"Your car sure likes gas," the man said.

"It has every since I bought it," I confessed. "But in the old days when gouging was reasonable, I thought nothing of putting in a half tank and whizzing around the Beltway without a care in the world. Now I think twice about going to the Dairy Queen. Will you check the oil and wash the windshield?"

"For a lousy hundred dollars worth of gas! You drivers are always looking for something for nothing."

Hard Facts about Soft Money

AMERICANS ARE GETTING more and more cynical about their elections. They believe that money buys politicians, and those who give the most get the most back if their man wins. It's more complicated than that.

The system works as follows: No individual can give more than $1,000 to a candidate. But any trade organization, labor union or corporation can give unlimited amounts to political parties that can use the money to finance the candidates of their choice.

The dollars that interest groups shower down are called "soft money." It looks and feels like hard money, but when you spread it around it smells more like political fertilizer.

I have *Time* magazine to thank for these numbers.

Bob Dole got $975,149 from Philip Morris. If you jump to the conclusion that Dole would become a pro-tobacco president just because of these donations, you are wrong. Bob has always been a pro-nicotine kind of guy, ever since he received free cigarettes in World War II.

RJR Nabisco gave $696,450 in soft money. The contribution was not to further its cigarette business but to protect its Oreos and Fig Newtons. Dole heard the message and has promised that, come hell or high water, he will keep the Food and Drug Administration from meddling with the cookie business.

AT&T contributed $352,000 and Atlantic Richfield $282,172. Once again this was soft money, but neither the phone industry nor the gasoline industry has any interest in getting favors from a Republican administration.

Brown and Williamson Tobacco gave $265,000 and Archer-Daniels-Midland Co., which controls most of the grain sales in the United States, donated $255,000. But you don't have to worry that Dole will make a payback if he becomes president.

I am happy to report that the Democrats are not accepting soft money for political reasons. They took $1.8 million in 1995 from the trial lawyers, which is no big deal. Why the heavy donation from this profession? Well, Hillary Rodham Clinton is a lawyer, as is the president, and when it comes to soft money you have to support your own. As one lawyer explained it, "The contribution was an investment because we'll get it back from all the Whitewater trials."

The Democrats also got a $303,480 donation from AT&T, $292,750 from MCI Communications and $215,250 from Anheuser-Busch.

These are just a few of the soft-money contributions made. They don't give any idea of how many actual dollars are being raised by the parties to elect their candidates. We're talking about fund-raising dinners and what people are paying to rub shoulders with President Clinton and Bob Dole. Each rub over $10,000 translates into a future favor.

Both parties deny that soft money guarantees access to the government. "We only accept the money because people want to give it, and if we don't take it, their feelings will be hurt," a soft-money collector told me.

"We could run this campaign without contributions from the lobbyists, but it would take all the fun out of it for the donors. It would also mean that Dole and Clinton might never have an opportunity to meet the people who can really help them run the country."

A Lust for Politics

WHAT SURPRISED ME THE MOST about Dick Morris's alleged romance with a $200-an-hour "significant other" was the revelation that they shared all the Democratic secrets. Apparently Sherry Rowlands was turned on by politics, and one can only speculate on their pillow talk at the Jefferson Hotel.

Here's my guess:

Sherry: Oh, darling, come to bed and tell me what you brought as a gift for me.

Dick: The latest polls from California. We're climbing back up after the Republican convention.

Sherry: Oh, don't stop—don't stop.

Dick: Things are looking good in Florida and Texas, and the commercials are starting to pay off in Oklahoma.

Sherry: Hold me close, my darling, and tell me we're going to win in Kentucky.

Dick: Kentucky *and* Arkansas.

Sherry: Is it true what they say about Al Gore?

Dick: What do they say about Al Gore?

Sherry: I was watching Ted Koppel while I was waiting for you tonight. Ted said Al Gore is stiffer than the Washington Monument, but the voters like stiffness. Jack Kemp is almost as stiff but in a supply-side-economics sort of way. I want you desperately, Dick, but before we embrace I have to know more abut Clinton's entitlement plan.

Dick: Move over, and I'll whisper in your ear. We are not going to touch Social Security or Medicaid.

Sherry: Oh, darling, never stop saying that to me.

Dick: I pushed the president to sign the welfare bill.

Sherry: Only you, Dick darling.

Dick: I get my kicks every time Clinton raises the minimum wage.

Sherry: When you say things like that, I just want to swoon.

Dick: Would you like to read the president's acceptance speech?

Sherry: I'm afraid I'll go crazy and scream if I do.

Dick: That's what I like about you. You're the only woman I know who goes ape reading a Clinton speech.

Sherry: Dick, I can't believe my eyes. It says here that Clinton is going to balance the budget in seven years.

Dick: He wouldn't say it if it weren't true.

Sherry: Oh, Dick, please seal that promise with a kiss.

Dick: I think I'm going to have to get back to the White House soon. How much more pillow talk would you like?

Sherry: I want you to stay here with me forever.

Dick: I'd love to, but I still have to worry about Pennsylvania.

Sherry: Dick, do I mean more to you than Michigan's electoral votes?

Dick: A lot more. Why do you think I keep coming back?

Sherry: Tell me if I mean more to you than New Jersey.

Dick: Sherry, I love you, and love means never having to
           say you're sorry, even if the tabloids find out we are
           messing around.

Daddy's Little Drill Sergeant

AS SOON AS THE VIRGINIA MILITARY INSTITUTE voted to
accept women at the school, a version of the following scene took
place among alumni all over the state.

"Alice, I have good news for you. You can now enroll in VMI,
my alma mater, which I have loved all my life."

"Daddy, I don't want to go to VMI. I want to go to Radcliffe."

"Shame on you. Radcliffe is for girls."

"But I am a girl."

"VMI will give you the steel and discipline that your brother
and I have. I have dreamed of this moment for years. The fact
that you can now enroll is an opportunity you can bless the
Supreme Court for. Just think. You'll be the first Donahue woman
to attend VMI, and your daughters and granddaughters will follow suit. I can't wait for you to be a brother rat."

"Dad, I read that they are going to shave the heads of the
female cadets to teach them a lesson."

"You won't be sorry. One day when you're in the trenches of
Malaysia, you will thank VMI for shaving your head. You will also
understand that they had to shave your head to wash your
brains."

"Daddy, I really don't want to spend my college years doing push-ups."

"Bite your tongue. Everyone has to do push-ups. You can't fire missiles at the Iraqis if you are unable to flex your muscles. VMI is the perfect school for you."

"If I can't go to Radcliffe, can I go to Smith?"

"They don't teach you character at Smith. VMI is the only institution where they instruct you on how to throw yourself on a live hand grenade and win the Medal of Honor."

"I was hoping to become an interior decorator, not a war hero."

"I'd hate to see you waste your life drawing pictures of living rooms when you could be on a twenty-nine-mile hike with only one canteen of water and cold C rations. That's what I always envisioned for my daughter."

"Daddy, I appreciate you wanting me to attend your alma mater, but I am not a chip off the old block. I believe in the military, but not as a career for me."

"But I've already sent off your application. You get special treatment because I was in the top ten percent of my class. I can't very well cancel the application. It would be a cowardly thing to do."

"I'm not going. I am not interested in carrying a rifle around and eating VMI food. I don't want to prove that I'm better than a man when it comes to running the obstacle course, nor do I want male cadets chewing me out because my shoes aren't shined."

"I never thought a daughter of mine would reject the opportunity to learn how to deal with mental strain, physical stress and psychological pressure. You've let me down, and you let my school down. You'll have to live with this for the rest of your life."

"Sorry, Pops, but maybe you can come visit me if I go to Sweet Briar."

"Doesn't any young southern woman care about going to Somalia anymore?"

The Great Portender

OUR LONG NIGHTMARE of another presidential campaign is almost over. Since I am somebody who knows what the future holds, my phone has been ringing off the hook with calls from readers wanting to know who our next president is going to be.

After studying my polls and checking out what will happen in Idaho, my prediction is that we'll have to stay up until seven o'clock on election night before any of us can start humming "Hail to the Chief."

Here's where we are right now.

Before they pull the lever, voters still have to make up their minds whether President Clinton is the head of a Colombian drug cartel or Bob Dole is in cahoots with the nicotine wranglers from Marlboro Country.

As I see it, the key factor in the election that could turn it around is if Bob Dole would join Ross Perot's campaign and help Perot's third-party chances of winning the White House. Dole has nothing to lose at this stage, and, while the two men don't get along, accommodations to travel on the same bus could be made.

Bob Dole's only argument for voting for Bob Dole is that he will keep foreign money out of American politics.

So far the American people don't seem to be bothered by Clinton or Jesse Helms taking money from abroad. As one Democratic fund-raiser said to me: "We give everybody money for their elections. It's about time some of it came back."

One thing rattling Dole is that the liberal press won't write about Clinton's peccadilloes. Clinton's spokesman responded, "That's nothing but politics."

Which takes care of that issue.

Dole may possibly have made a big mistake when he asked the American people to wake up and see what was going on in the country. The voters from my polls resent his asking the question when he was the one who put them to sleep in the first place.

Something else that could affect the outcome of the campaign in the hours before the polls close would be if Al Gore spoke out and Jack Kemp shut up. But the main question we must ask ourselves is how many people will actually vote? People also wonder: If Bob Dole had started his hard-hitting, below-the-belt politics earlier, would Chelsea Clinton still be ordering new drapes for her room at the White House?

And so as we prepare to say *au revoir* to the last presidential election of this century, I will make my fearless prediction: In spite of a liberal press and lying spin doctors on both sides, the election is too close to call.

Trust me.

Cuppa Coffee

THE BEST CUP OF COFFEE in Washington can be found at the White House. Its reputation is such that people from all over the world stop by to share a cup of java with the president.

These klatches attract businessmen and lobbyists from the Far East who will do anything to own a mug bearing the presidential seal.

While the coffee is always excellent, it is not necessarily cheap. A good cup of Jamaican blend costs anywhere from $134,500 to $200,000—not including sugar.

People who complain about the high prices are told that the president's coffee goes through a certain filtering process—its secret known only to the Democratic National Committee.

Besides, what you get with your coffee is the president of the United States, who will listen to your story, whatever it is.

At these prices, the question is often asked if a visitor gets doughnuts as well. Those who have attended the klatches say that anyone who gives more than $200,000 is entitled to as many doughnuts as he wants. A spokesman said, "The president always claims that coffee without doughnuts is like a day without sunshine."

How did the White House become so famous for its coffee? One day an Indonesian businessman from Arkansas stopped by, and Clinton offered him a cup of mocha java.

"How much is it?" the businessman asked.

"There's no charge for my coffee," the president said. "I don't want to make a profit on my brew."

An aide standing next to the president whispered to the overseas visitor, "If you'd like to donate $150,000 to buy a new coffee pot for the White House, we'll take it."

The businessman plunked down the money, and the president poured him another cup of coffee. Another venerable tradition was started.

Pretty soon word got out in the Far East that the best coffee klatches in the United States were being held at 1600 Pennsylvania Avenue. When they heard the news, Malaysian businessmen were prepared to kill for a cup of good American coffee. In order to keep the president from being overwhelmed with visits from coffee lovers, a minimum cover charge of $120,000 would be levied on each cup. This didn't seem to bother the Taiwanese, the Thai, or the Chinese businessmen who sold arms to the mainland.

When one Thai merchant was questioned as he left the White House with a Bill Clinton mug, he said, "What's the big deal? Someone has to finance an American election."

Tell It Like It Is

YOU SEE IT IN ALMOST EVERY NEWSPAPER STORY: "Mr. Squab (or whatever his name is) was not available for comment," or "Mr. Squab refused to talk to this reporter."

As more and more wrongdoers refuse to talk to the media, reporters feel rejected and wounded.

Stanley Fischer told me, "I don't understand it. I make a call to Squab, and I'm very polite on the phone, and I tell him I want to discuss his dalliance with a married female jockey at Belmont racetrack, and he won't talk to me. Do you know what he said? It was none of my damn business."

"He shouldn't have said that. After all, you are a newspaperman, and it is his duty to discuss his misbehavior with you."

"That's what I told him. I said we knew he was fooling around in Louisville during the running of the Kentucky Derby, and it would be better for him if he came clean."

"What did he say to that?"

"He wanted to know who said he should come clean. I told him it was my business and the public's right to know. As a newspaperman I am obligated to write the truth, the whole truth, and nothing but whatever else happens when somebody is messing around."

"You said the politically correct thing. The Supreme Court gives newspapermen the right to question other Americans about what happens behind their closed doors. I would hate to live in a country where people keep secrets from each other."

Fischer said, "You know Carole Garbus, who says she was checkmated by an Argentine chess player in a Beverly Hills hotel?"

"I don't know her personally."

"Well, I called her this morning to have her spill the beans to me, and she referred me to her lawyer. It's disgusting the way they treat the press."

"There should be a law that makes it mandatory to talk to someone from the *National Enquirer*," I said.

Fischer replied, "I don't want to be in a profession where people accused of being up to no good treat you like dirt."

I said, "I remember the days when subjects talked to the press because they were afraid if they didn't the reporter would write something awful about them. Now those you call won't speak at all."

Fischer said, "It's not the same business it used to be. Instead of people facing a scandal head-on, they'd rather hide behind drawn window shades and give us the finger. My question is, if they make themselves unavailable to the pen, how do they expect to avoid us sticking them with a sword?"

It's All Legal

WHILE DEFENDING HIS ROLE in the Democratic fund-raising controversy, Vice President Gore said that he had done nothing illegal, but he won't do it again.

Apparently, one of the vice president's duties was to make telephone calls to prospective contributors and shake their money trees.

What he actually said to these people is anybody's guess.

"Hi, this is Vice President Gore and I'm making a legal telephone call to you."

"This is an honor, Mr. Vice President. Why would you call me?"

"Because the president told me what a great American you are. He said, 'How I'd love to play a no-conflict-of-interest golf game with Philip Dellinger.' 'Why?' I asked the president. He replied, 'Because he hits the longest ball of anyone in Little Rock.'"

"When did the president say that?"

"Yesterday morning when he was having breakfast with eight Chinese businessmen and an arms dealer from Pakistan. It was all perfectly legal because we only served decaffeinated coffee."

"What do I have to do to play golf with the president?" Phil wanted to know.

"Don't cheat on your score."

"Could I make a donation to the Democratic Party?"

"We never mix golf with fund-raising. But if you would like to drop something in the eighteenth hole to help save this great country, we wouldn't turn you down, because our lawyers have assured us that it is legal."

"If I gave two hundred fifty thousand, would that be legal?"

"It would be more than legal. It would definitely be in the ballpark. However, the gift only entitles you to putting on the green with the president of the United States and taking one shower in the Lincoln Bedroom when the game is finished."

Phil said, "That sounds like something I'd enjoy doing. When can we tee off?"

"How about tomorrow morning before the president addresses a fund-raiser given by the Loyal Sons of Sultans of the Oval Office?"

"Great. Is there anything I should bring besides my golf clubs?"

"That's it. The Democratic National Committee supplies the balls. That's why it's all legal."

"What does the party expect from me after I donate two hundred fifty thousand?"

"Just be yourself, Phil."

Nearer My God

WHEN I WENT TO SEE the Broadway musical *Titanic,* I accompanied two ladies. At intermission they excused themselves to go to the powder room. Ashley returned in ten minutes—Stockard was nowhere to be seen.

"Where is Stockard?" I inquired.

"She's standing in line waiting to go to the powder room."

"How come," I asked, "you went at the same time she did and you're back and she isn't?"

"I went to the men's room. I crashed in and said, 'Sorry, boys, I can't wait in the ladies' line. Watching the *Titanic* going down is much tougher on a person's kidneys than *Phantom of the Opera.*'"

"Weren't you afraid that by using another sex's facilities you would be arrested?"

"What for? I didn't steal anything. You don't realize what a man's world this is until you have to stand in line with sixty-five other women waiting to powder your nose."

"What did Stockard say to you?"

"She said if the *Titanic* went down to save a place in a lifeboat for her."

"It sounds as if she was taking it well," I said.

"Except for standing on one foot and then the other, she was in good shape."

"When she saw you going into the men's room, why didn't she follow you?"

"She said she didn't have the nerve. She was fearful she would wind up as a headline in the *New York Post*: DEBUTANTE CRASHES MEN'S ROOM — MALE THEATERGOERS DEMAND THEIR MONEY BACK."

I said, "I hope she gets back before the owners of Macy's go down."

"Stockard told me if she doesn't make it back before the *Titanic* sinks to meet us in the parking lot and bring a piece of ice."

"Well, Ashley, I must say you did the right thing. There is no sense going to the theater and behaving like a lady. What is interesting, though, is that in the second act the orchestra is not playing 'Nearer My God to Thee.'"

"They are playing outside the ladies' room."

Smoke in Your Eyes

WHEN THE STORY BROKE that secondary smoke causes heart attacks, I didn't believe it. The report said that health risks were double for those victimized by other people smoking.

I had my doubts until I passed a large building on Madison Avenue where fifteen people were standing in the entrance puffing away.

I heard one smoker say to another, "How many did you get today?"

The other replied, "Four certain and two possibles. A smoker can't count a sure hit unless another smoker sees it."

A lady said, "I decked a man in an Armani suit yesterday who was carrying a Louis Vuitton briefcase. That should count for something."

"How did you do it?"

"I had my hand cupped around my Virginia Slim. He never suspected I was going to blow a smoke ring up his nose. He clutched his chest as he hit the sidewalk."

The lady standing next to her said, "Zelda, you've committed the perfect crime."

"They still don't consider secondary smoke a crime of passion."

I was about to walk on when I saw a man with a pipe in his hand. He pointed it at me. As far as I was concerned, he had a smoking gun aimed at me.

"Don't shoot," I cried. "I'm not antismoking."

He said, "Anyone who stands within two feet of a pipe smoker is dead meat."

"Puff away," I cried. "You have your rights."

The man next to him said, "Put your pipe down, Paul. If he says he likes secondary smoke, he must be a fruitcake."

I said, "You're good people, but how do you keep anticigarette zealots from spoiling your day?"

A man said, "It's all done with smoke and mirrors. You have to think of us as the Cosa Nostra, and you have to imagine the nonsmokers as wimps. Every time someone complains about cigarettes, we feed them to the fishes."

I was impressed. "No wonder Philip Morris stock is going up."

I Do

SINGLE MOTHERS HAVE MORE PROBLEMS getting married than other people do. I discovered this when I was witness to a proposal by a friend of mine named Jim, who said on bended knee to a friend of mine named Bonnie, "Will you marry me?"

Bonnie was taken by surprise. "When?"

Jim said, "It doesn't matter—it could even be at your convenience."

Bonnie, a single mother who has two children, said, "Well, I can't do it this week because I promised Nick's class I would drive them in a van to Montclair, New Jersey."

Jim said, "But I love you very much. And want to live with you the rest of my life."

"And," said Bonnie, "I want to live with you the rest of my life except for next weekend when I am taking all the kids to see *The King and I*."

Jim was desperate. "Let me take care of you and make you happy and convince you that all men are not rotten."

"It sounds like bliss, but it will have to wait until Kathy is fitted with all her braces. She hates dentists."

Jim said, "I love children. I'll take good care of them."

"Nick does not like men touching me."

"Even after we're married?"

Bonnie said, "We could do it when the kids go to the movies. That way it won't cause trauma."

"Are you sure you want to marry me, Bonnie?"

"Of course, I'm sure, but let's not make any plans in July when I have to go visit my mother in Nantucket."

Jim got off his knees. "Maybe we should think it over."

"There is nothing to think over. You love me and I love you, and we could get married in September before school starts and I don't have to carpool."

"Will we have time for a honeymoon?"

"We'd have a week if I can get my sister to take care of our cat."

Part Four

Questions, Nothing but Questions

WHEN THE LEADER OF THE FREE WORLD visits Martha's Vineyard, he brings with him a battalion of press corps people who have been assigned to file interesting daily stories about the island. Most of the reporters are completely ignorant about Martha's Vineyard and depend on residents like myself to provide journalistic enlightenment.

I received my first call at 7 A.M. from a staffer on a Miami newspaper.

"How big is Martha's Vineyard?" he asked.

"It's about the size of England," I told him.

"What is the staple diet of the inhabitants?"

"Their main source of protein is avocado dip and nacho chips washed down with gallons of California Chardonnay."

"What is the income of the average summer resident?"

"Ten million dollars, which is immediately invested in a lawn sprinkling system."

"What kind of currency does the population use?"

"It's called the Moped. Somebody will say, 'I'll give you four Mopeds for a fat-free ice-cream cone,' or, 'If you give me ten Mopeds, I'll give you enough gas to get you to Gay Head.'"

"What are the traditional ways of the summer people concerning their offspring?"

"Each day they place them in tiny sailboats and ship them out to sea, telling them not to be late for dinner."

"Why do you think President Clinton likes Martha's Vineyard?"

"Because Ken Starr spends his summer in Galveston."

"How do the other island inhabitants feel about the president coming here?"

"It doesn't bother them as long as the Secret Service personnel don't eat up their supply of sweet corn."

"What do people on the Vineyard talk about?"

"They're certain that Elvis is on the island, but nobody knows if he rents or owns. We also talk a lot about whether Chelsea should have gone to VMI instead of Stanford, and there is lengthy discussion over whether the Vineyard should be declared a smoke-free island."

"Do the island people get upset when the president comes?"

"No, they only get upset when their houseguests arrive."

Wherefore Art the Prez?

MARTHA'S VINEYARD — It goes without saying that everyone on Martha's Vineyard wants to see the president.

Nobody wanted to see him more than Luke Larson.

Larson's neighbors back in Toledo knew that Luke was on the island, and if he didn't see the president at least once he would turn out to be one of Toledo's stumblebums.

The night Clinton arrived on the island Luke rushed out to the airport, only to discover that he had missed him by ten minutes. He watched tearfully as the president and his entourage disappeared down a dirt road.

His wife told him, "Why don't you go to the golf course tomorrow morning? He's sure to show up."

Luke got up at 5 A.M. and went out to Farm Neck Golf Course. He set up his portable chair and started on his doughnut and coffee. By eight o'clock there were hundreds of people standing around, hoping to get a glimpse of the prez.

In the distance Luke could see four figures surrounded by Secret Service men advancing toward a fence. Just at that moment a man on a large motorized lawn mower yelled at the crowd, "Please move out of the way—I have to cut the grass."

Luke yelled, "But the president is coming."

"That's why I have to mow the lawn now. He doesn't want to lose his ball."

Everybody moved away from the fence, and no one caught so much as a glimpse of Mr. Clinton.

Luke was so discouraged that he went home for a bowl of clam chowder.

His wife said, "I hear that Ted Danson and Mary Steenburgen are giving a birthday party for the president's fifty-first. Maybe you could see him from the road in Chilmark."

Luke let out a triumphant yell, dashed out of the house and drove up South Road. He parked his car, climbed onto a roof and tried to peek over a stone wall. Nothing. Then he heard sirens and ran to the side of the road. In front of the presidential vehicle was a TV truck with a cameraman on the roof. It completely obscured Luke's view—all he saw was the side of the truck with the lettering: CHANNEL 5 — ALL THE NEWS WHEN YOU WANT IT. When he got back to his car there was a parking ticket on the windshield. The fine was $50.

Feeling dejected, Luke went home and took a hot bath.

The next day he heard that the president was going boating. He went down to the dock of the Edgartown Yacht Club only to discover that the boat had been moved to the Vineyard Haven Yacht Club.

This made him sick. He walked home and said to his wife, "That does it. I'll never give a hundred thousand dollars to a Clinton campaign again."

Break-In

ALTHOUGH THE TOBACCO INDUSTRY is putting up a valiant effort, occasionally it loses one. Somehow, no one knows exactly how, it managed to slip into our tax-cut legislation a $50 billion tax break for tobacco producers.

The tax break was squirreled into a bill to underwrite health care for children. It was offered at the last moment so that there would be no debate and discussion. To this day, no one knows who introduced the bill.

This is one theory of how it wound up there:

Four plumbers wearing ski masks—two from the tobacco industry and two senators from southern states—broke into the Budget Committee hearing room with the bill to give the tobacco people a tax break.

One of the men took the health-care-for-children bill and tacked the tobacco interest law on the end of it. "That should do it. No one will be able to find this with all the garbage that the budget bill is full of."

A masked senator said nervously, "Suppose someone finds it and they vote to repeal it?"

"You are worrying for no reason. No one is going to discover a tobacco tax break in a bill this large. Frankly, I think we should insert a rebate of more than $75 billion because it might be the last tax break we have."

The other masked senator said, "I always like to sneak in a bill when no one is looking. I once got the Senate to approve an Air Force base in my home state when they were voting on a bill to eliminate scarlet fever. Getting something you want for something you couldn't care less about is what makes Congress a great legislative body."

One of the tobacco industry plumbers said, "I can't get our tobacco bill to stick to the budget bill."

"Did you try Scotch tape?"

"Yes, and even Elmer's glue. Senator, you are going to have to introduce an amendment to this bill guaranteeing a windfall for the people who make cigarettes."

"I would be honored." He raised his hand over the bill and said, "I hereby propose a fifty-billion tax-relief amendment for anything that has nicotine in it."

The other senator said, "I second the motion."

All four plumbers said, "Aye."

The bill was rolled up and put on the Senate majority leader's desk where it rested until someone came across the wording and raised Hades.

An antismoking senator voiced his objection and demanded a repeal of the tax break.

It was agreed to 95 to 3.

The four plumbers met that evening to drown their sorrow but were cheered up by a tobacco lobbyist who said, "There is always tomorrow night."

Belly-Up

Question: Why did stocks go belly-up on Wall Street recently?

Answer: Nobody is quite sure. The experts believe that Bu Fang, a big investor in Hong Kong, was suffering from kidney stones. In excruciating pain, and not wishing to live, he screamed, "Sell, sell, sell."

His broker did. When Singapore traders saw the sell-off in Hong Kong, they panicked and began to unload blue chips, which sent the Bangkok exchange into orbit and drove Tokyo dealers to commit hara-kiri.

Word reached Germany, then London and finally the United States, where the greatest financial minds in the world, most of whom live in Connecticut and New Jersey, were shaving. When they arrived at their offices, they all came to the same conclusion: "If Hong Kong was selling, something was rotten in Denmark."

From then on all Hell broke loose in Brazil and Argentina with everyone selling and nobody buying.

Q: Did a lot of people lose a lot of money?

A: It depends on what you mean by a lot of money.

Most of their losses were not their own money. For example, if you'd bought stock at $100 and it had reached $500, you could either say that you lost $400 or that you still had your $100. People who thought they had lost $400 tried to jump out the window. Investors who felt that they had broken even went to the movies.

Q: What about the little guy?

A: Whenever anything happens in the stock market, Wall Street blames the little guy. If stocks go up, the soothsayers say that the little guy was finally getting into the game. If stocks go down, they say that the little guy was chickening out and causing a recession.

Q: What about the big guy?

A: Big guys don't panic. All the big guys are playing with other people's money. They don't feel good about losing OPM, but they don't feel bad enough to stop taking their families to dinner.

Q: The financial playing field is now global. Do you see a problem in that?

A: It depends on what the Estonian brokers decide to do with Sri Lankan bonds.

Q: Will the market come back to its previous level?

A: It could very easily if Bu Fang passes his kidney stone.

Four Score

IT IS NOT GENERALLY KNOWN, but Abraham Lincoln taped all his conversations in the White House. He told his staff, "I want to go down in history as the great emancipator, and the only way I'm going to achieve that is if all my conversations are recorded."

Richard Morris, who was advising the president on political issues, said, "Mr. President, we need money for your election, and we're not going to get another nickel out of the fat cats until we offer them something more exciting than a sleep-over in your log cabin in Illinois."

"What do you suggest?"

"We have to open up the White House to the big givers."

"You mean a tour?"

"No, they should be invited to stay overnight."

"Where would we put them?"

"How about the empty bedroom overlooking the Ellipse?"

"What would be such a big deal about letting a donor and his wife sleep there?"

"We could tell them it's the room where you slept. Why don't we name it the Lincoln Bedroom? Nobody would be allowed to sleep there for less than one thousand, which would be the equivalent of two hundred and fifty thousand in 1997."

"Okay, but let's not take any Confederate money because people will say the South is trying to buy the election."

"Gotcha. We need to create a package for givers. Mr. President, how about you playing golf with the big donors?"

"I don't play golf. I don't have the clothes for it. But I am willing to take them to Rock Creek and let them watch me split rails."

"That's great. Why don't you and the First Lady treat everyone to an evening at Ford's Theater?"

"I don't know if the play is any good."

"We're talking about the presidency of the United States, sir. We can't afford to lose the election because of a lack of funds. A recent poll from Atlanta said that only one percent of that region's population approves of your policies. We're going to have to plaster the town with billboards to change their minds. We propose that everyone who gives ten thousand to the campaign gets a briefing on the war by Ulysses Grant."

"Okay, but keep him away from the bar."

"Mr. President, the vice president has to help us. I suggest that he go to the homes of potential donors and explain why we need the money."

"Is that legal?"

"As long as he doesn't do any campaigning from inside the White House."

"What else?"

"This is the biggie. If someone gives more than ten thousand he will be invited to watch Robert E. Lee surrender at Appomattox."

Where Are My Socks?

WHEN THE HISTORY OF the Clinton administration is written, its epitaph might be: THEY COULDN'T FIND ANYTHING. Never have so many items been lost by so few.

An example of this came to light several weeks ago when the president was dressing for a state dinner, and he said to Hillary, "Where are my socks?"

Hillary responded, "I haven't seen them. Are you sure you had some?"

I thought I did," said the president. "I'll call my legal counsel." He picked up the phone. "Did I have black socks in the chest of drawers in my bedroom?"

"None that you have to worry about, sir," came the reply.

"I need them for the state dinner tonight."

The lawyer said, "I'll have my people search for them, although I hate to take them off their regular job. They have been so busy answering subpoenas for a smoking gun that if they have to look for your socks they'll fall behind."

Mr. Clinton said, "Okay, call the FBI. Maybe they can find my socks."

"With all due respect, sir, I don't think we should call the FBI. They may not find your socks, but they're bound to find something else we don't want Janet Reno to know about."

Hillary was getting nervous. "Maybe you could borrow a pair from Al Gore."

The president said, "I don't want him to know that I can't find my socks. He might lose respect for me."

"Yes, but you promised to let your vice president in on everything in case he had to take over the presidency at a moment's notice."

"I'm sure they're in the White House somewhere."

Hillary asked, "Did you look on the third floor?"

"Why the third floor?"

"Because that's where everything we lose is usually found."

"I'll send the housekeeper there." Mr. Clinton looked anxiously at his watch. "But the Chinese premier is almost here. I have no choice but to greet him without any socks on."

Hillary said helpfully, "If you stand up all evening nobody will notice."

The president was about to go downstairs when the housekeeper came rushing in. "I found them, sir."

"Where?"

"Between the Rose law firm's billing records and the White House tapes of you having coffee with the Hong Kong soccer team."

Danger: Reading Materiel

THE THING THAT MAKES Ken Starr a great prosecutor is that he will subpoena anybody, anywhere, to track down one of his usual suspects. Even if it's a manhole cover, he'll demand it be produced for the grand jury.

The latest to be subpoenaed is Kramerbooks, a bookstore in Georgetown. Starr demanded it turn over a list of books that Monica Lewinsky had purchased there.

I'll be very honest. I had no idea this had anything to do with Whitewater, and it made me slightly nervous when I went into a bookstore the other day.

Everything seemed natural, except that all the salespeople had "FBI" printed on the backs of their blue jackets.

Smelling a rat, I said to one agent, "Do you have *Rebecca of Sunnybrook Farm?*"

The salesperson handed me a copy. When I handed it back to him, he started to dust it for fingerprints.

Curiosity got the best of me, and I asked the clerk what was up.

"We got a tip that Monica Lewinsky may have bought a copy of *The Joy of Sex* here last week, and we're checking it out."

"What would happen if it was confirmed?"

"It would be another damaging clue to help Ken Starr in his case against Monica's mother."

"Are people indictable because of the books they purchase?"

"It's up to the judges who are monitoring the Starr investigation."

"Will I be subpoenaed for buying *Rebecca of Sunnybrook Farm*?"

"It depends if you bought the hardcover or the softcover, and whom you bought it for."

He told me, "*Rebecca of Sunnybrook Farm* does not entitle anyone to executive privilege. But that isn't what we're looking for. If Monica bought a book titled *Vox*, which deals with people having phone sex, it's a serious offense and worth the thirty-six million it's costing the taxpayers for the Whitewater investigation."

"I don't want to go to jail for buying a book," I said.

"You should have thought about that before you riffled through the Constitution."

Viagra, the Politically Incorrect Pill?

IF SOMEONE WERE TO ASK ME what was the greatest invention of the twentieth century, I would reply without hesitation: the drug Viagra, the cure for impotence.

For the first time in human history man no longer has to fear striking out when he is expected to hit a home run.

It goes without saying that I don't need Viagra (FBI testimonials supplied by sending a self-addressed envelope), but my friend

Barney's life immediately changed for the better when Pfizer put it on the market.

The first thing Barney did was ask his doctor if there was any downside to the medicine.

His doctor said, "You can have a heart attack."

Barney said, "I'll take it."

The introduction of Viagra to the public presents very serious social problems. The question is, if you cure men of impotence, will that mean there will be more sexual harassment in the workplace? Will the pill give men who have no lease on life a new beginning and the promise of a rainbow in the sky?

I'm not discussing the help that married people will get from it. My fear is that the pill will fall into the hands of single men and terrorists who would use it to satisfy their own selfish, politically incorrect agendas.

There was a time when men asked women if they were on the pill. Now, women must ask men the same question, and if they both say yes, the obvious next question is, "Your place or mine?"

Pfizer should put warnings on its Viagra label: "This pill may only be used by consensual people. Use without permission of both parties could lead to high blood pressure and astronomical legal fees. The pill is not a cure for the common cold but should give you the same feeling of well-being produced by Prozac or Polident."

I happen to be a supporter of Viagra and, like so many other people, I regret to this day that I did not buy stock in Pfizer.

Obviously, it's a drug whose time has come—or at least the time has come to take this drug.

It's now up to the American people to decide what to do with the weapon—just as they had to decide what to do with the atomic bomb. The only evidence I have that it works is from Barney. Ever since he took Viagra, he has had a big smile on his face.

Armed and Dangerous

EVERY TIME YOU TURN ON the TV news, you see groups of well-armed men in different countries shooting at one another. The thought must occur to others, as it has to me, "Where do these people get their lethal weapons?"

Don't look farther than the United States, which is the biggest merchant of death in the world—twice the size of any other major power. Some figures show that it sold $11.5 billion worth of weapons last year—up 23 percent from the year before.

Ordinarily this would not present a problem except that there are conflicts of interest within our government. For example, the Pentagon sells enough guns and war supplies to set the capital of any nation on fire. The State Department's role is to extinguish that fire.

The conversation between the two goes something like this:

The deputy secretary of peaceful negotiations at the State Department calls the deputy secretary of Pentagon big bangs and says, "I hear that you just sold ten million worth of land mines and flamethrowers to the Republic of Doggerel."

"Yes, we did," says the Pentagon secretary. "It was a tough sale because Doggerel terrorists wanted nuclear warheads on their flamethrowers and so did the government troops they are fighting."

"See here, we've been working for a cease-fire in Doggerel for three years, and since both sides were running out of ammunition, we almost had it. Now with a new supply of weapons they will be at each other's throats again."

"The Pentagon does not allow peace negotiations to interfere in its arms sales program. Our job is to get rid of everything we have so we can buy more equipment. Without our big-spending customers we would be a third-rate power."

"Why have you sold so much stuff to the Middle East?"

"You ask the dumbest questions. We always give buyers what they want if they pay cash."

"Even Iraq?"

"Why don't you people at State get real?"

"Because some of us over here believe that selling fighter planes to China can disrupt relations with India. This could eventually force us to intervene and send our troops into Bangladesh."

"It doesn't matter what you believe. Our arms clients are our friends, and we'd rather they, and not the other side, have our weapons."

"What other side?"

"The one that just bought our helicopters."

You'd Better Cooperate, or Else

MY FRIEND JOSEPH HELLER wrote a classic war novel titled *Catch-22*. The story had to do with a bomb squadron in Italy. Anyone who is crazy does not have to fly the dangerous bombing missions. But if you say you don't want to fly the missions, then obviously you are sane, so you have to fly them. Catch-22 has become part of the English language.

I thought of it the other day when I read that the Supreme Court ruled you can't execute a killer if he is insane. You can kill him only if he is sane. So the object of the state is to cure the man so they can kill him.

I am not making this up. The court ruled seven to two that killing someone by lethal injection when he doesn't have his wits about him is cruel and unusual punishment.

The mission of the state is to get the psychiatrists to work on Ramon Martinez-Villareal's sanity.

Let us go to the death chamber where Ramon is sitting in his cell surrounded by psychiatrists.

"Ramon, we're asking you to be reasonable."

"Babble, babble, babble."

"You're pretending you're insane just because you want to live. We all know you're faking it."

"Babble, babble, babble."

"Ramon, why won't you take your medicine? This is the latest pill for schizophrenia, and it has been successful in sixty percent of our cases. Just try it. It doesn't have any side effects."

"Babble, babble, babble."

"If something bothers you, tell us. We wish to hear about it. We don't want you to go to Heaven with any anxiety."

"Babble."

"Oh, come off it, Ramon. You're just a spoiled murderer who is refusing to pay your debt to society. Would you be averse to taking electric shock? If it works, then we can get this silly business over with."

"Babble, babble, babble and more babble."

"Oh, shut up. If you keep babbling we're going to report you to the warden, and he'll put you on bread and water."

"Obscenity."

"I think he's got it. By Jove, he's got it. Now repeat after me. The rain in Spain is mainly on the plain."

"Cock-a-doodle-doo."

"Well, he had it a minute ago. As far as I'm concerned, you're a lot saner than you pretend to be."

High Crimes and Misbehavior

I INTEND TO TALK about alleged adultery. The only reason I wish to discuss it is that it's a major topic of conversation at beach parties and cookouts in the United States.

Alleged adultery is not committed by as many people as you think, but at the same time it is committed by more people than we all like to admit.

Ken Starr is determined to hang the president of the United States because he allegedly committed adultery and lied about it. Monica Lewinsky is also accused of committing alleged adultery and, depending on which way she goes, also could be hanged for indulging in the sport.

The question raised by the public is whether committing adultery is in the same class as conducting a nuclear test over India.

It is generally accepted that the only way to deal with adultery if you are caught is to deny it. We know all the stories about the husband getting caught with a woman and saying to his wife, "Now, don't believe what you see."

American culture demands that, when caught, neither party admits to any hanky-panky. Occasionally there are tearful confessions of bundling, but as long as both parties stick to their stories, no one gets in trouble.

What we have in the Starr case is a zealot who is determined to send anyone to jail for allegedly having had one or more escapades.

As far as we know right now, Starr has nothing to charge except that Monica Lewinsky allegedly was playing spin the bottle with the president in the Oval Office.

Let us, for argument's sake, say that it is true and there was a relationship between Monica and the president. What does it all mean? The stock market is perking along, interest rates are down and a theater ticket on Broadway only costs $75. We, the taxpayers, are hoping Starr is wrong and will be disbarred.

I am not going to serve on any jury that tries Monica Lewinsky for any adulterous high crimes or misdemeanors.

Like Starr, I believe confession is good for the soul, but when it costs us $43 million for what goes on behind someone's closed doors, it's a real bargain.

Washington Water Torture

OKAY, SO KEN STARR LEAKED evidence to reporters, not to gain an advantage in his investigation but, he said, to "set the record straight."

Besides, Starr's defenders say, the White House is also leaking to the press, so Starr has to fight fire with the truth.

The real truth is there is so much leaking going on in Washington right now that reporters are wearing life jackets when they go to work.

How does a story get leaked when there is a "mum's the word" order from the judge?

This is how it is done. Most leaks are by phone, though some are tossed over the office transom at night or sent by fax to a media source's home.

The phone rings in a columnist's office. "I can't tell you who I am, and if you say I told you anything I'll deny I ever said it, but Monica Lewinsky had a serious crush on Jim Carville and used the president to get to meet him."

"Holy Linda Tripp. This is dynamite."

"I'm only telling you this to set the record straight."

A second method of leaking is to send the leaker to a restaurant like the Palm, where all the media big shots hang out.

The White House leaker will sit at the table next to someone like Sam Donaldson and say in a loud voice, "We have a list of all the books Ken Starr bought at Barnes & Noble, and when we give it to the grand jury they'll bar him from every library in America."

Sam, of course, takes the bait, and immediately calls Cokie Roberts on her private line.

The most high-level form of leaking takes place when someone from the special prosecutor's office of the Justice Department leaves a microfilm of the grand jury testimony under Lincoln's big toe at the Lincoln Memorial. The leaker notifies the leakee when to pick it up.

The beauty of leaking in Washington is that no one has to check out the facts. All the leaks come from either a "reliable source" in Starr's office or a Chinese lobbyist in Arkansas who "refused to take our calls."

From Charlton to "Chainsaw"

EVERY SO OFTEN, two or three news stories break at the same time, and I feel obligated to deal with all of them at once.

This time, Charlton Heston became president of the National Rifle Association, the Southern Baptists ruled that a wife must graciously submit to her husband, and the chairman of the Sunbeam Corp., known as "Chainsaw Al" Dunlap, was bounced out on his ear by his board of directors, and his golden parachute didn't open.

First, the Charlton Heston appointment. Moses, or Ben-Hur, or whoever he says he is, indicated he was taking the job so people will stop knocking his beloved guns.

It isn't guns that do the damage, Heston says, but the fact that the courts are not enforcing the laws.

Moses is a firm believer in the Second Amendment and doesn't like schoolchildren shooting schoolchildren any more than their parents do. At the same time, you cannot penalize law-abiding citizens just because a kid is going to lose it when someone at school calls him a name.

Where do the Southern Baptists come in? They come in by ordering their women to submit to their husbands.

How does that fit in with Charlton Heston? It's yet to be spelled out, but I might be bold enough to suggest that if a wife does not submit to a husband, she should be shot.

I'm not saying that this be done by a member of the NRA, but they should have first crack at the target.

My last story has to do with "Chainsaw Al." The reason he was named "Chainsaw" is that he constantly bragged about coming into a firm and firing thousands of workers to drive the company's stock up.

While doing this *and* losing money for Sunbeam, Al kept shooting himself in the foot, which Heston maintained that he had a constitutional right to do.

When "Chainsaw" got the boot it was revealed he worked out a $35 million severance package for himself. Instead of 35 million bucks, the board of directors gave "Chainsaw" a semiautomatic pistol and told him to do the right thing.

It was a great day for Charlton Heston and husbands of Baptist women—but people at his company say "Chainsaw Al" has seen better ones.

Don't Let the Bedbugs Bite

THE STARR CHAMBER CONTINUES. Just when you thought it was safe to go into the water, the special prosecutor bites your leg off.

The latest leak by CBS News is that Ken Starr intends to question Secret Service people on Clinton's sleeping habits in the White House. Starr wants to know how Clinton knew he was asleep and when he knew it.

I will now take you to the grand jury room where Jack Conner, a Secret Service man, is being questioned.

"Mr. Conner, where are you stationed in the White House?"

"Under Mr. Clinton's bed."

"All night?"

"Yes, until he gets up in the morning. My job is to see that nothing happens to the president when he has his eyes closed."

"Do you also watch Hillary Clinton when she is in bed?"

"No, a Secret Service woman is assigned to watching her."

"And this agent is also under the bed?"

"Yes. It sounds a bit crowded, but that's what we're paid for."

"Does the president talk in his sleep?"

"He does sometimes. He says things out loud such as 'Long live the people of China in the Year of the Rat' and 'Republicans suck eggs.'"

"Has he ever talked about Monica Lewinsky?"

"I don't believe that name has ever come up on my watch."

"Did Mrs. Clinton ever bring it up?"

"You'll have to ask her Secret Service woman."

"Does the president sleep in pajamas or without sleepwear of any kind?"

"Why do I have to answer that?"

"Because we have to get to the bottom of Whitewater, and we'll never be able to do it unless we find out what Clinton wears at night."

"He sleeps in pajamas."

"Don't you find this weird?"

"When you're a Secret Service person, nothing is weird anymore."

"Mr. Conner, does the president ever walk in his sleep?"

"Not to my knowledge. He sleeps soundly, as if he hasn't a care in the world."

"Well, this is hypothetical. Suppose he did. What would you do?"

"I would follow him."

"If he committed a high crime or a misdemeanor while walking in his sleep, would you report it to the special prosecutor?"

"That's what we're paid for."

It Only Hurts When I Call the HMO

EVERY YEAR THERE IS A PARTICULAR INDUSTRY that gets people mad at it. This year it is the for-profit medical plans that are making it more complicated for clients to get their health care.

In the beginning the health insurance companies seemed to be the solution to all our problems. On one side were the executives, who were willing to bet their policyholders that they wouldn't get sick. On the other side were the policy owners, who lived in deathly fear that they would.

At first the profit-making health insurers insisted they were there only to serve the public. As time went on they admitted they were really there to serve the stockholders.

To make a reasonable profit, new rules were issued, and the bureaucracy became worse than it is in the IRS.

This is why the public is now biting its fingernails.

"Can I help you?"

"Yes, I am a member of the Newpain Beneficial Health Insurance Plan. I would like my tonsils removed."

"Who said you should have it done?"

"My doctor."

"What does he know? Before we pay for it, you will have to talk to Miss Clara Foradyce in our second-opinion diagnosis department."

"Who is she?"

"She's our expert medical chief, and all tonsil operations have to go through her."

"Is she a doctor?"

"No, she previously worked in an animal hospital and gave shampoos to dogs and cats."

"I don't see why she should decide whether I should have a tonsillectomy or not."

"Listen, buster, we're not in this business for our health. We can't make money if we have to okay the removal of every Tom, Dick or Harry's tonsils."

"But your advertisements say you will keep me well in sickness and in health."

"A good policyholder doesn't get sick. A good policyholder doesn't keep calling up our busy staff with some ridiculous medical problem. We prefer our customers to cure themselves through faith healing."

"That's pretty good, but on the off chance that my tonsils may start hurting, can I come back to you and have you reconsider paying for the operation?"

"You can do anything you want to, but I'm warning you, Miss Foradyce hates to be second-guessed."

Starr Search—A Fee for All

THE THING I LIKE MOST about Ken Starr is he doesn't care how people spend their money. In his fishing expedition he is forcing not only the major players in his investigation to recruit high-priced lawyers but also innocent people who are not even involved in the case.

Take Simpkins, the pastry chef in the White House. He works in the kitchen and has never met the president or Monica Lewinsky or even fed scraps to Buddy.

Starr has decided Simpkins should testify against the president and reveal the recipe for his chocolate éclairs, which possibly were eaten by Lewinsky.

Starr's lawyers tell Simpkins if he doesn't testify he will be making rye bread for the rest of his life on the mothballed battleship *Missouri*.

Simpkins goes to his superior, who tells him, "You better hire a lawyer. I would never appear in front of the grand jury without legal advice."

"How much will that cost?"

"Probably twenty-five thousand dollars."

"But I don't have twenty-five thousand dollars. I'm just a pastry chef."

"You should have thought of that before you made éclairs for the president."

Simpkins raises the money by selling his mother's house.

His lawyer tells him, "Now that you are a witness, you're going to have to hire a bodyguard and rent a bulletproof sedan."

"But I didn't do anything, and I don't know anything, and I didn't see anything."

"What has that got to do with hiring a good defense lawyer?"

"This is ridiculous. Isn't there any law prohibiting me from being called?"

"You don't want to be called?"

"I don't want to pay twenty-five thousand dollars for no reason. If I knew what it was going to cost, I would have committed a much bigger crime than baking a birthday cake for Hillary Clinton."

"Starr just wants to touch all the bases. How can he say he investigated Whitewater thoroughly when he hasn't subpoenaed every person in the White House?"

"Does your fee include everything it will cost to represent me?"

"Not the appeal I'll eventually have to make for you to the Supreme Court."

A Poor Excuse for a Leader

IT WAS THE FIRST MEETING in Moscow between Boris Yeltsin and President Clinton. The ruble was lower than the Moscow subway.

Yeltsin said to the president, "I'm up to my ears in fiscal borscht. What do I tell my people?"

President Clinton said, "Tell them the truth. They'll forgive anything if you tell them the truth."

"But my devaluation plan didn't work. The country is going broke."

"It doesn't matter as long as you level with your people. They expect you to make a few mistakes. After all, leaders of super-powers can screw up. But if you go on television and offer a mea culpa, they will say, 'Let's get on with it.'"

Yeltsin said, "What's a mea culpa?"

"You go on television and ask everyone, including God, to forgive you for your sins."

"Will it work?"

"It always works for me," Clinton said. "I had a problem recently, and I was being criticized for it. So I told the country I had made a slight mistake, and afterward everyone was glad I admitted to it."

"Will they forgive me for defaulting on my loans?"

"They forgave me when I said I had defaulted on personal matters, and everyone breathed a sigh of relief. In our country they like a president who is a straight shooter."

"Suppose I devalued the ruble, defaulted on my loans and had an affair with a ballet dancer in the Kremlin. Should I confess to all three?"

"Two out of three is enough. The Russian people don't want to hear all your mistakes."

Yeltsin was grateful. "I feel terrible about the ruble falling. At the beginning I denied that it had fallen. But then the evidence kept piling up, and I was sure people would not believe me. The Russians get upset about their rubles."

"You did the right thing, Boris. Never explain and never complain. Swearing on a stack of rubles usually works when all else fails."

"Will my confession help me in the polls?"

"It helped me. I was way down in the polls until I told the truth about Hurricane Bonnie on CNN."

To the Moon, Ken! To the Moon!

SPACE. WE ARE STILL THRILLED WITH IT, provided a seventy-seven-year-old senator from Ohio is in the capsule. John Glenn was our biggest hero when he went up in space in 1962, and he is our biggest hero now that he has done it again.

But Glenn's feat is more than going up and coming down. John is a twofer hero, and we don't get many of them anymore. When he returns, brokers on Wall Street will stop buying stock so they can take the time to tear up ticker tape to throw out their windows.

The first part of space flight had to do with worldwide coverage of the event—including the voyage to the moon.

The second part was coming home again and being greeted at the White House and having a glorious return to the Rose Bowl parade. Most of the astronauts could handle the flight part of the mission. It was the PR duties that took their toll on our mission pilots.

John Glenn was not the president's first choice to go into space. President Clinton always wanted Ken Starr to fly in the shuttle, but Paula Jones's lawyers protested, and Starr could not get the approval of the hundreds of grand juries he represented. So it was decided to send Newt Gingrich up for nine days just at the time of the elections. James Carville said this was a risky decision, so he recommended John Glenn, a loyal Democrat, who could fly by the seat of his pants with the House Judiciary Committee.

The big factor was age. If Glenn could do it, it would be a big boost for mankind and the voting bloc of Medicare and Social Security. Once the choice had been made, the president had to talk Glenn into returning on a mission. "The country needs a hero now more than ever, John. It could be you or Michael Jordan."

Glenn was at first reluctant. "Sir, I'm not sure I have the right stuff."

The president smiled and said, "I thought that about myself when I first became president, but I was persuaded that when the going gets rough, all of us have the right stuff."

The man the president had chosen was the right man for the right job. Ken Starr may have been a younger choice for the mission, but he was much too serious to hop around in a spacecraft.

The president said, "Now that Glenn has accomplished his mission, we have to start thinking of somebody else to grasp the imagination of the American people. Hillary will accept no one else but Walter Cronkite."

When Your Friends Are Really Bugged

MRS. MACINTOSH WALKED INTO her daughter Blossom's room and found her taping a Radio Shack recorder to her hip.

"What are you doing?" Mrs. MacIntosh asked.

"I plan to tape-record my best friend, Mona," Blossom replied. "Why?"

"All the kids are doing it. It's the only way we can get the goods on our buddies."

Mrs. MacIntosh said, "But that's dirty pool. You're not supposed to record your best friend."

"She says she's having an affair with the principal. But I have no proof of it. If I can get her to talk, I'll have everything down for the Parent Teacher Association."

"But it's so unseemly."

"Mom, don't you understand what it is like in the real world? People talk, but it's rare that anyone has corroboration. Mona tells me everything."

"Like what?"

"Whenever she is sent to the principal's office for misbehaving, he makes a pass at her. He also buys her presents, and she calls him Big Bozo. If you heard the tapes, you'd agree they're spellbinding."

"Blossom, it's against the law to tape another person without her knowledge."

"When they hear my tape, I'll get immunity."

"Isn't there any way I can convince you that what you're doing is a very bad idea?"

"I doubt it. Tape-recording is like smoking—once you start, it's impossible to give it up. Mona said that tonight she is going to tell me how the principal made her get him an egg salad sandwich when she was sent to his office for punishment."

Mrs. MacIntosh said, "I don't want to be a party to this. In our day you didn't tape your friends. You shared confidences with them. That is what they were there for."

"Mona would tape-record me if she had the opportunity."

"All right, do what you want to, but I hope you don't get caught."

"I won't. No one can see the microphone in my hair."

"You have it all thought out. Where did you learn all this?"

"I've been watching Linda Tripp. She is a role model to all of us."

"The kids like her?"

"Is Elton John British?"

Santa, Looking to Close a Sweetheart Deal

IT HAS JUST BEEN ANNOUNCED that the Christmas season will merge with Valentine's Day in one of the greatest financial deals of all time. Originally, Christmas tried to merge with Hanukkah, but the Grand Rabbi of the North Pole turned it down.

So Santa Claus, the CEO of Christmas Inc., looked for another likely prospect and found one in Valentine's Day.

"It's a perfect fit," said Santa. "We both deal in love. They are strong in greeting cards, and we are big in Barbie dolls."

The price was $40 billion. North Pole Christmas executives said there would be a big cost savings when they laid off those who worked at Christmas and Valentine's Day factories. "We don't need the number of reindeer that we have used in the past," an executive vice president said. "We also intend to buy our mistletoe from China and load our sleds with more eau de cologne from Taiwan. Christmas will be a slimmer but more successful holiday, and our profits are expected to soar."

The people at Valentine's Day are not as happy. A Cupid doily maker told me, "Everyone knows that Christmas gobbles up everything. Valentine's Day will lose its meaning when the Christmas executives start cutting back on expenses.

"Lovers are very sensitive people, and you can't treat them as you would the customers at Toys 'R' Us."

A maker of chocolate truffles said, "The merger doesn't make sense—Christmastime leads to greed—Valentine's Day to affection and tenderness. We're heart specialists. All Christmas thinks about is the bottom line."

There is some question as to whether the Justice Department will permit the two holidays to merge. An antitrust attorney said, "I don't know if we are talking about restraint of trade or not. The Christmas people would like to have Americans spend all their savings in December. The Valentine holiday people have only one big moment in February, and that is when everyone goes to Hallmark. The concern is that if Christmas owns Valentine's Day, they could start marking up all the greeting cards, and with a monopoly on love it would no longer be dog-eat-dog."

Santa angrily denied the charge that the merger would destroy competition. "We're not trying to monopolize the holidays. Our only intention is to cut down on our labor costs. We can save billions of dollars if we dump enough people at Christmas.

"We also can be more efficient. We'll offer two bouquets of roses—to be sent at Christmas and Valentine's Day—for the same price.

"We have to accomplish this merger so we can compete with the Chinese New Year."

Santa was asked what holiday Christmas would merge with in case the Justice Department would not allow him to buy Valentine's Day.

"We'd join up with Halloween. It's become a real moneymaker."

Surprise Witnesses

IF THERE IS TO BE AN IMPEACHMENT TRIAL—and there probably will be—the public will expect a few surprises. They are inured to television dramas, when, at the last moment, a witness or a piece of evidence is suddenly produced to save the defendant.

There are some scenarios I have in mind as to what would make a satisfying climax to a dreary proceeding.

At the last moment, just as Henry Hyde is summing up, Paula Jones dashes into the courtroom and says, "I made a mistake. It was the other Bill Clinton who owns the Little Rock Car Wash. I beg the president's forgiveness for putting him through this horrible ordeal, and I am giving him back his eight hundred thousand dollars."

The Senate unanimously votes Not Guilty.

Or perhaps there could be this version:

The White House counsel says, "If it please the court, we have a surprise witness who can shed light on this case—Mr. Samuel Eckstrom of the Pennsylvania Avenue Dry Cleaners."

"Mr. Eckstrom. Tell us your story."

"I was cleaning this dress of Monica Lewinsky's when I accidentally spilled Elmer's glue on it. I tried to get it out, without success, so I sent it back with a note and a check from the insurance company for fifty-nine dollars and ninety-five cents."

Senator Lott says, "This puts an entirely different slant on the case."

A final ending to this episode that would satisfy everyone
would be when a White House lawyer rushes into the Senate
chambers just as Strom Thurmond is summing up. "Your Honor,"
he addresses Chief Justice Rehnquist, "these papers were just
found in a pumpkin in Philadelphia. They were left by our
Founding Fathers. They say they would never consider phone sex
a high crime or a misdemeanor. It was the Founding Fathers' wish
that such a charge, if made, be immediately dropped and the
president be fined thirteen dollars and fifty cents."

After hearing the convincing evidence, the Senate, by a voice
vote, shouts, "NOT GUILTY!"

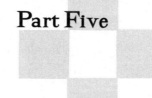

Part Five

Even Friendlier

THERE IS GOOD NEWS from the friendly skies of United. It has just announced it is giving its top coach passengers five to six more inches of legroom than they had before. This will not be available to everybody—only frequent flyer club members and those who pay full coach fares.

Everyone is rejoicing. This is a real breakthrough, particularly for people who have leg problems. In the past, many of our airlines have requested that people check their legs in the baggage compartments above their seats. Those with particularly long legs were requested to check their legs at the terminal curb and pick them up when they arrived at their destination.

United said it will have a special section set aside to provide its favored people with legroom. Those who are in the back of the plane will still be required to hold their legs up against the passenger in front of them.

Instead of "Smoking" and "No Smoking," the lighted signs will indicate which sections offer room for your knees.

The question arises, how did United arrive at giving us the whole five to six inches of extra space? My guess is they put a passenger in a flight simulator and tested what would be a reasonable area for him without causing too much animosity with the poor coach passengers who were lucky someone would even sell them a ticket.

An interesting thought occurred to me and that is, was United admitting by their move that they were not providing enough leg space to economy class? We all know that economy-class passengers, based on what they eat, do not demand much compared to those in first class.

United says it is catering to the legroom class because most of the complaints have come from businessmen whose companies won't let them fly first class.

Doctors for the airlines say that most passengers in economy have enough legroom if they sit on their legs and don't try to stretch them.

United is the first to give their customers a break. Reports indicate that the other airlines will match them. As one plane designer said, "We consider this one small step for man and one giant step for mankind."

I'm not a chronic complainer, but I believe everyone—man, woman and child—should be entitled to six inches of leg space. If Lindbergh had flown with the leg space the airlines give our economy passengers, he never would have made it to Paris.

Trashing Virginia

THE GOOD NEWS FOR VIRGINIA is that there are strong indications that they will soon receive New York's trash.

While the contract has yet to be signed, the decision is almost in the bag.

Many states were vying for the tons and tons of waste, and Virginia environmentalists were thrilled to win the contest.

One Richmond trash booster told me, "It's like winning the Olympics. For New York to bestow this honor on us when there are so many places vying for their garbage is a waste management dream come true."

What made the state one of the favorites is that New York has supplied Virginia with 60 percent of its trash in the past.

The selection team said this was a factor because Virginia knows how to handle trash. They are skilled in separating bottles from cans and paper from *Hustler* magazine. The New York Trash chairman said, "We made a personal visit to the site, and we discovered Virginia dumps are everything they claim to be. Only New Jersey has better trash dumps, but we would have had to wait until 2006 to get an empty site."

I raised the question—which was natural after the Salt Lake City Olympics scandal—of whether Virginia officials had bribed anyone to get New York's waste.

The answer was "No. The fact that the New York committee received free tickets to Williamsburg is strictly coincidental."

"Was any trash traded for sex?" I asked.

"Not that we know of. But sometimes you can't separate one from the other."

One of the major complaints of Virginians is that if they keep accepting out-of-state garbage there won't be any room left to dump their own.

New York's reply is "They're talking about apples and oranges."

Bill Gates and Me

BILL GATES HAS JUST WRITTEN a book entitled *Business at the Speed of Thought,* in which he has listed the "Ten New Rules Concerning Computer Networking."

Without stealing his thunder, I also have ten rules that I will eventually put in a book. They are not as sophisticated as Mr. Gates's are, but, then again, I don't have his money:

1. When turning on your computer, try to remember your password. Many people cannot boot up their machines because they can't recall if they named their password after their wives, their children or the girl next door.
2. Do not hit any key you are not certain of, as it will only make you lose the file on your hard disk. You may ask, "Which key?" No one knows which button on your computer will make you lose everything you have written for the last two days.
3. Spilling coffee or Coca-Cola on your keyboard will cause more trouble than the drinks are worth.

4. Do not put a computer in a microwave oven if it does not warm up.

5. If you have difficulty getting the font you want, do not call the computer maker to talk to someone. They will put you on hold for three days until you starve to death.

6. There is no such thing as a friendly computer. It will stab you in the back as soon as you turn to answer the telephone.

7. A computer is so simple even a child can use it—as a matter of fact, ONLY a child can use it. Do not try to do anything on a computer unless someone under thirteen is standing next to you.

8. The more bells and whistles a computer has available, the less chance you have of doing anything on it.

9. The Internet is as good a way as any to say "Hi" to people who live in New Guinea.

10. There is no way of getting rid of an outdated computer other than to get in your car and drive it to a salt mine in New Mexico.

The Polite Police

THE POLICE IN NEW YORK CITY have been ordered to be polite. They are now even carrying cards that tell them what to say to the citizens. Mayor Rudy Giuliani maintains if the police are more polite, then the city dwellers will react in kind.

I've set up several situations that might happen if everyone is nice to each other.

"Sir, were you thinking of holding up this bank?"

"Yes, Officer. That is what I had on my mind."

"If you did that, I would have to arrest you and bring you to justice."

"I agree that it will put you to a great deal of trouble, but as John Dillinger once said, 'A bank is the only sure place where the money is.'"

"Sir, what had you planned to do with the gun you are holding in your hand?"

"I was going to use it to frighten the employees."

"That's not a good idea. It's against the law to point a gun at people and frighten them. If you did so, I would have to read you your rights, which include hiring a lawyer—and you know what they charge these days. It's more than you can get from robbing the bank. If you will excuse me for a moment, I just saw someone go through a red light."

"Forgive me for asking, but why did you go through a red light?"

"That's a dumb question. I went through the light because I didn't see it."

"That's nothing to be ashamed of, sir. Many of us spend our lives not seeing red lights."

"You are a very understanding policeman."

"All New York City policemen are understanding. We feel people's pain. If you'll excuse me, I see several gentlemen stealing a BMW from the curb."

"All right. Please put that car back where you found it. Don't you know it's a crime to take someone else's transportation in the confines of New York City?"

"We didn't know that, Officer. We thought if you found an automobile on the street and it was unoccupied, it was yours."

"You've been misinformed. I must charge you with car theft."

"Okay, but I have a right to make one telephone call. Do you have change for a dollar?"

"Here is a quarter from my own pocket. I pray the person you are calling is in."

Surfing for Pleasure

I WANT YOU TO KNOW what I do best is surf the channels on television. I can sit in front of the set and in one minute examine every show on the air.

The reason I bring it up is that there is a controversy raging as to how much damage the TV shows can do to young brains. What is wrong with the debate is that no one is discussing what it does to grown-up minds.

The other night I was surfing in my favorite chair. The first program I hit was a man throttling a lady on the roof of an empty warehouse. The attacker was wearing a ski mask and didn't seem to be a friend to the woman.

I pushed the button on the clicker. A dozen gang members were in a parking lot, firing submachine guns at each other. If this wasn't enough, one group poured gasoline on the other and set their opponents on fire.

I was hoping to find some less violent action, so I hit the clicker again. I saw our planes bombing Belgrade. I would have stayed with it, but I'd seen it before.

The next click found me in the jungle with a crazed snake attacking an innocent baby.

I asked myself, "What has Mother Nature come to?"

The thing that surprised me was how many women heavies are involved in violence on TV. They had the weapons and they had the time. The prettier the girl, the more people she was able to wipe out.

The only difference between the male shooters and the female markspersons was that the women hid their Colt .38s in their brassieres.

I remembered that I was paying for a sports channel that could give me some relief.

I surfed to it only to find a hockey game in progress and both teams beating the hell out of each other as well as the referees.

The only nonviolent television on that night was wrestling, because everyone knows it is not for real.

Does TV cause people to do violent things? I don't think so. Shooting another person is something someone will do whether he sees it on the tube or not.

Garroting and other crimes of violence cannot be blamed on Hollywood.

When you see someone pushed out a window and he goes splat on the sidewalk, "That's Entertainment."

Don't Touch Me

SINCE THE SUPREME COURT RULED that a woman may sue if she believes she has been harassed, men have been wary of making moves that would bring them in front of a grand jury.

Delilah Frescoe recently came into my office. She was about to shake hands with me when I asked her to leave the door open. I said, "Legally, I can't touch you with a ten-foot pole."

"Why?" she asked.

"I'm just playing it safe in case this visit turns out to be an abusive one. What can I do for you?"

"I came to you because I have a problem. I'm in love with Charles Killdair, and he is in love with me."

"Then what's the problem?"

"He won't touch me. He is afraid I would accuse him of sexual harassment."

"That's ridiculous. You wouldn't do that, would you?"

"No, but Charles's brother is a lawyer, and he advised Charles to play it safe."

"How can Charles show his affection for you if he won't touch you?"

"I asked him the same question and he said that he would do it verbally, and I could reply in kind."

"I assume this is not satisfactory."

"Well, it leaves a lot to be desired. A girl likes to get kissed once in a while if she's in love. I offered to sign a statement saying that I wouldn't sue him if he held me in his arms at the movies."

"And what came of that?"

"Charles's brother said it wouldn't suffice if someone reported us to a special prosecutor."

I said, "If Charles really loves you, he would take a chance even if it means ten years in prison."

"I don't know how much passion he would put into kissing me if he knew it could lead to perjury."

I told her, "This is a tough case. People have to show affection for each other if they are in love. That's what all the songs are about. Have you spoken to your lawyer about this?"

"Yes. He advised me not to make the first move on Charles. If Charles wants to kiss me, we should find a third party to witness it. If he wants to go even further, we would ask five or six people to look on. They can testify if it was consensual, and that both of us were trembling at the same time."

This was a difficult case. I told Delilah, "The rules of love are different from the rules of the court. There are only two choices: You're either going to have to find a fiancé who is not afraid of getting physical or one who doesn't have a lawyer for a brother."

House for Sale

THE CLINTONS ARE LOOKING for houses in New York. Some areas don't care who you are—others are intent on knowing more about the potential buyers.

So it is with Happy Valley Shangri-La, which has a committee to interview prospective buyers.

"Mr. Clinton, is there anyone who can recommend you for this purchase?"

"I'm sure Ken Starr, the lawyer, will send a letter. He has always spoken highly of me."

"Mrs. Clinton, can you tell us why you want to buy a home in Happy Valley?"

"I want to be near my ancestors. They all lived in Scarsdale."

"Mr. Clinton, is there anything we should know about you that you haven't told us in your application?"

"My life is an open book. I have never made anything up."

"Mrs. Clinton, is there anything we should know about Mr. Clinton that he hasn't told us?"

"I've said all I want to say about that in *Talk* magazine. Look, we're just two simple people who want a nice home where we can sit on the porch and count our blessings and legal fees."

"We're not badgering you, Mrs. Clinton. What makes Mr. Clinton believe he can take care of a two-million-dollar house in Happy Valley?"

"He ran the entire United States for eight years, and it has never been in better shape."

Mr. Clinton says, "I launched seventy-five cruise missiles at Kosovo and Iraq. That in itself should guarantee how much I care about private property."

"Bill doesn't like to be pushed around," Mrs. Clinton adds.

"Mr. Clinton, have you ever been involved in an inappropriate relationship with anybody we know?"

"If you mean have I ever had a platonic golf game with somebody, the answer is NO. That's why I want to live in Happy Valley, where everybody minds their own business and has cookouts in their own backyards."

"Mrs. Clinton, do you have any political ambitions?"

"I'd love to be president of the Happy Valley Garden Club. But I know you can't achieve something that big overnight."

"Hillary is good with people," Mr. Clinton says.

"What attracted you to Happy Valley?"

"What attracted me to Happy Valley was that every house looks like the White House."

The head of the board says, "Our architects are known for their imagination."

Mr. Clinton asks, "Is it all right to build a presidential library?"

"As long as you don't build it in the front yard. Well, Mr. and Mrs. Clinton, it looks like you pass the test. You'll be happy to know we have bingo every Friday night."

Is There a Doctor in the House?

IT ISN'T AS EASY TO SEE A DOCTOR as it used to be. I discovered this when I received a message from Doctor Kastner last week. He wanted to see me to check up on something or other.

I called the next morning and told the nurse that Dr. Kastner wanted to see me.

She said, "How about November fifteenth?"

"That's good," I said, "but since he wants to see me, could we move up the date?"

She said, "Just a minute. How about November tenth in case we get a cancellation?"

"Has the doctor any plans for me if something happens between now and November tenth?"

"Most of our patients have to wait longer. I'm squeezing you in because you have health insurance."

"This is my problem," I told her. "I know after the doctor checks me out he's going to send me to a specialist. When I call the specialist he will tell me that he can't see me until December thirtieth. So, in truth, I won't see the doctor for two months."

The nurse said, "Everyone has to take his chances. Dr. Kastner may send you to a different specialist to check you out with X rays. In that case, we'll have to get you an appointment with the lab. The last time I tried that, they couldn't see anyone until the summer."

"Thanks a lot," I said, and hung up.

Then I started to think about my condition. I knew there was nothing wrong with me at that moment, but Doctor Kastner can always find something that needs to be looked into. That's why I figured he would want to see me in October.

So I called back and said to the nurse, "This is Mr. B. Did anything open up since I spoke to you a few minutes ago?"

"Let me check. How does November third sound to you?"

"Sounds okay. It will be great to see the doctor."

"It's not an appointment to see the doctor. It's for blood tests. Also, don't eat any breakfast on November tenth and bring somebody to drive you home."

"No problem," I said. "And I'll see the doctor that day?"

"He's attending a conference in Fort Lauderdale. I have to reschedule everyone. Can we talk about November twentieth?"

"Of course we can. I'll try to stay well until we do."

Time and Time Again

AS MORE AND MORE TV MAGAZINE SHOWS take to the air, there is a desperate search for notorious criminals to appear on them. We're not talking about the run-of-the-mill convicts who committed ordinary crimes that hardly made the newspapers.

The producers are searching for those criminals who have committed heinous acts, which will boost the shows' ratings.

I talked to one of the top TV magazine executives in the business.

"Why do you keep putting long-term inmates on your show?"

He said, "Because they can't charge us for coming on the air. We're always looking for free talent."

"You had a stalker on TV last week who was doing fifty years, plus life. He seemed to enjoy being interviewed. Is there any danger that you were fulfilling his fantasy of becoming famous for fifteen minutes?"

"That's not why we do it. We interview the top criminals in the country because our audiences are fascinated by those who are paying their debt to society. We only want top-of-the-line cons on the show. As a matter of fact, a lot of the criminals have agents who alert us to their clients. I was offered a serial killer yesterday who was abused by a schoolteacher when he was a child, and committed all sorts of crimes. NBC and CBS were after him, too, but he always watched our show and offered to plead guilty to be on it."

I said, "It must cause a lot of havoc when you book one person on death row and turn down the other nine."

He replied, "You have to be tough in this business. After all, you can't let feelings interfere with your ratings. Almost every person in jail believes he should not be there. But once he's there, he's certain he should be on television."

He continued, "Last week I heard from a talent agent who wanted to book his star arsonist who was in solitary confinement in Sing Sing. I had to turn him down because we can't seem to get an audience for arsonists."

"Don't you think you created a monster by having to put so many noted criminals on your show every week?"

"For a while we did not have access to the biggies. But the courts ruled they had a right to tell their story like everybody else. We didn't know what we had until a sniper who had shot up a drive-in theater won an Emmy for 'Best Acting by a Performer Doing Life Without Parole.'"

Where Are You, Norman Rockwell?

WHAT I MISS THE MOST around Thanksgiving time are the Norman Rockwell covers on the *Saturday Evening Post*. Let's face it—the Norman Rockwell Family at Thanksgiving is gone. They have been replaced by the 1999 Nonnuclear Family.

In the Norman Rockwell Family there were the mother, the father, grandpa and grandma, and the little tykes, all standing around admiring a beautiful roasted turkey. Everyone was there to show us what a real American holiday was all about.

But alas, the Norman Rockwell Family has disappeared and been replaced by the Nonnuclear Family. Here is how it is shaping up:

The Bomeisters are having the dinner, but Gerald Soda (the eleven-year-old son of Mrs. Edna Bomeister, who is divorced from Gerald's father, Jim Soda) has to go to his father's home in Nantucket. But it's a wash because Jim's second wife has to send her child to her ex-husband in Montana.

Ed Bomeister intended to bring his widowed mother for Thanksgiving from Seattle, but she now has a boyfriend and will spend the holiday with his family. Edna Bomeister's mother, who lives in Sun City, Arizona, couldn't come because she was unable to get a frequent-flyer airplane ticket. Airlines don't like to give free tickets around the holiday season.

Bomeister's brother, Bubbie, at the last moment said he had just busted up with his wife and would like to come to Ed's for Thanksgiving. Edna thought she was being taken advantage of, but there was nothing she could do, as Bubbie not only had lost his wife but also had just been downsized at the warehouse by Wal-Mart.

The Tennysons, who live next door, told Bomeister that both their college students were going skiing and would not be home for Thanksgiving.

They decided since they were alone to go to a restaurant. Ed invites them.

If everyone had kept to their schedule, there wouldn't be a problem, but things started to unravel when young Gerald Soda's plane to Nantucket was canceled. Mr. Soda was furious and said he was going to take Mrs. Bomeister to court as she had violated the court decree.

At the last moment the Tennyson college kids changed their minds, decided to come home and told Mrs. Tennyson they were bringing four friends with them.

Mrs. Bomeister couldn't get a final count, so she ordered a turkey and a ham. This was barely enough after she found out that Ed's boss was coming with his new girlfriend.

I keep wondering how Norman Rockwell would paint this Thanksgiving dinner. I am certain everyone wouldn't be smiling at the turkey.

His famous cover of the Thanksgiving family still sells. People want to remember what a real family gathering was all about. I know Norman would have gotten a frequent-flyer ticket for Ed's mother-in-law. Also, Mrs. Bomeister would have made her own stuffing instead of buying it at the store.

Ed's brother would be in the picture with his wife after their reconciliation, and the Tennysons would be shown with their children and four friends carrying in pumpkin and apple pies.

Little Gerald would not have to go to Nantucket because in Norman Rockwell's world there would be no divorce decrees that would make him go somewhere else on the holiday.

Norman would present the Bomeisters as a happy, functional family, ready to dig into the turkey and sweet potatoes.

It's a Thanksgiving without glitches, and as warm and tasty as the holiday itself. It is no wonder that now in American households, when everyone is at the table, the older generation says to the younger one, "You should have been there."

Health Tips

THE FIRST TIME MY TENNIS ELBOW started acting up, I remembered I had seen an advertisement for a cure in *Time* magazine. I went down to my magazine dealer, Louie, and when he found out why I wanted to buy *Time* he said, "That's Pheladelrin. You can't buy it without a prescription. On the other hand, *Newsweek* is advertising Betamotomotor. But they say it isn't for everybody. Some people who have taken it have had their fingers fall off."

I asked Louie, "What would you recommend for tennis elbow?"

"*The New Yorker* has a six-page spread on T-scalpin. But the ad says you can't buy it unless three doctors want to give it to you."

"What about *Vogue* magazine?" I asked him.

"They're featuring a French drug called Quelle Chance. It not only can cure you but it will make your hair grow again."

"Louie, you're really up on these prescription drugs."

"You have to be if you're in the magazine business. Ever since the prescription drug companies started advertising products you can't buy over the counter, we news vendors have become essential to the health care of the public. The first thing I do when the latest magazine comes in is check it out and see what the cure for an ailment is. For example, a fellow came in for a lottery ticket the other day and started complaining because he had a terrible migraine headache. I immediately prescribed a copy of *Playboy* magazine, which was advertising Platopain Plus."

"Did you hear if he got the medicine?"

"His doctor wouldn't give it to him. He said he preferred the painkiller being advertised in *Vanity Fair.*"

"You really provide a public service," I said.

"I love what I do. If I can find a cure for asthma in *Bride* magazine, I'm happy."

"Are there any side effects to the medicine being advertised in *Newsweek?*"

"There are always side effects to prescription drugs. Besides your fingers falling off, in some cases you wind up with Lyme disease, contracted from ticks that live on the cotton in the bottle."

"What's the antidote?"

"I believe it's advertised in *Money* magazine."

I told Louie, "The problem with finding a satisfactory drug in a magazine is that you might also find a better drug advertised on television."

"My doctor is very careful about what he prescribes. He makes sure when he gives somebody something from *Good Housekeeping* that it does the job better than what they're pitching on *Monday Night Football.*"

Why George Can't Read

I'M NOT AS DISTURBED as most Americans are that George W. Bush did not know in a TV quiz who is in charge of Pakistan, India and Chechnya. While most of us learned this in public school, Bush was just out driving around and having a good time.

There is nothing in the Constitution that says the president has to know who the leaders of those three countries are. The reason is that presidential ignorance is not as big a problem as some people think. If you become president, you can hire people to tell you the names of the leaders of any country in the world.

Do you think President Clinton knew who was in charge of Chechnya? Not by a long shot. It doesn't matter. He was only a telephone call away from his secretary of state, Madeleine Albright, who had the names of every head of state on her Rolodex.

Some think that Bush had prepared himself for an interview on a Boston television show by learning the names of the leaders of Uganda, Tanzania and Yemen. He had their names written on the cuff of this shirt, but he was thrown a curve by the Pakistan and India question.

It is true that Pakistan and India are constantly changing governments and even people who appear on the TV show *Jeopardy* can't keep them straight. In Pakistan the rule of thumb is as soon as you make general you can take over the country.

Governor Bush had to live with his ignorance during the entire campaign.

To make things fairer, I propose that anyone running for president only be required to know the names of three prime ministers of countries of his choosing. While most would choose Great Britain, France and Monaco, the candidates who know the big shots from the Third World nations would be considered by the electorate to be much more qualified to run our foreign affairs.

Politics is a dirty business, and you have no idea what you're going to be asked when you go on TV. If you blow it, the press, who has nothing better to write about, will jump on you.

Not knowing the leader of Chechnya is unforgivable, and yet, 40 percent of our fourth-graders are just as ignorant.

What Mr. Bush has to do is rewrite his briefing book.

When an interviewer asks, "Who is the president of Ireland?" his response would be, "I can't tell you that but I can tell you who the leader of Taiwan is. It's Lee Ching-hua."

"You have just won two hundred dollars. Would you like to go for a thousand?"

"Yes, I'll try education."

"How to you feel about prayer in school?"

"Lee Ching-hua."

"Now one more question. If elected, whom would you appoint as the chairman of the Federal Reserve?"

"Lee Ching-hua."

In conclusion, every presidential candidate has an Achilles' heel. Bush can get his Chechnya indiscretion behind him only if he asks the American people's forgiveness.

Road Rage

ONE OF THE MOST POPULAR contact sports in the United States is "road rage." It is now played on the highways and byways of the country.

The great players are those drivers with short tempers who take out their anger on other cars. It used to be all verbal but it is now getting more physical, particularly amongst people who forgot to take their Prozac.

Donald Anchorman, who wrote the best-selling book *I Spit on Your Windshield,* told me, "Road rage now involves more people than baseball, basketball, football and hockey combined. It's also responsible for more ulcers and migraine headaches than any other sport. It used to take place only during rush hour, but now it is played day and night, even on secondary roads."

Anchorman said the game begins as soon as the driver is on the highway, and it helps if the person has just had a fight with his wife. Suddenly he realizes the vehicle in front of him is going too slowly. His first play is to put his hand on the horn. If this does no good, he passes alongside the car and shakes his fist at the driver. He also mouths some of the more familiar curse words. If this is not enough, the ultimate shot for the enraged driver is to stick his third finger up in the air at the other driver. This gesture is worth a thousand words.

Anchorman continued, "What makes road rage so exciting is when the other driver decides to fight back. Then you have two cars and two crazy people in play. They try to cut each other off or even hit the backs of each other's cars.

"By this time the other motorists on the highway have noticed what is going on. They pick up their cell phones and call nine-one-one. The Super Bowl of road rage comes when both the drivers signal to each other to pull over to the side of the road and punch it out."

I said to Anchorman, "This is a true story. A friend of mine named Blake spent ten years learning karate. He was on the highway in Los Angeles when a Porsche cut him off. Blake sped up and cut the Porsche off. The other gentleman then shifted into high gear and shot around Blake to cut him off again. Finally Blake pulled up next to the Porsche and motioned to the driver to get over to the side of the road.

"After ten years Blake thought the karate lessons would finally pay off. He pulled up on the shoulder in front of the Porsche. In the mirror he saw the driver get out of his car and walk toward him.

"Blake reached down to unbuckle his seatbelt. Unfortunately it wouldn't unfasten. While Blake sat there fighting with his belt, the other driver walked up and punched him in the face. Then he got back in his Porsche and drove away."

Anchorman said, "That is road rage at its finest."

Anchorman told me the only thing worse than road rage is "parking rage." This occurs when one person believes another has stolen his parking place. What makes parking rage so dangerous is that both automobiles are not moving. People have been known to go through the roof when they believe someone has stolen their spot.

There are now police reports coming in from all over the country concerning violence between parkers. People will fight to the death for their space. If they don't fight, it is the only time you will see grown men cry.

First Lady or Else

HILLARY CLINTON'S ANNOUNCEMENT that she is running for office has caused some difficulty at the White House. She is now wearing two hats—that of First Lady and also senatorial candidate for New York.

This is probably what is going on at 1600 Pennsylvania Avenue right now. Mrs. Clinton stops by the Oval Office to say good-bye to the president.

The president says, "Where are you going?"

"Brooklyn. They're having the Feast of Coney Island Day, and I have to have my picture taken eating a Nathan's hot dog."

"You can't do that. We're entertaining the president of Zanzibar tonight."

"There are no New York votes in Zanzibar."

"You have to stop thinking of your election, Hillary. After all, you are still the First Lady of the land."

"I'm doing as much as I can. I took the Boy Scout oath with Troop Forty-two of Schenectady in the Rose Garden last Wednesday."

"Hillary, people are starting to talk. The Daughters of the American Revolution have complained to me that whenever they want to see you in the East Room you're in Yonkers."

"My campaign staff says I have to take Yonkers if I ever hope to win Scarsdale. You made me launch a new aircraft carrier last month, and I had to cancel a photo op in Southampton."

"But Hillary, what hurts is that the newspapers don't print your picture unless you're campaigning in New York State. Let's make a deal. For every day you run for office in New York, you give me one day in Washington."

"That would lose me Buffalo."

"Look, Hillary. I'm still president of the United States, and people expect you to stand by your man."

"So what else is new?"

"You know the president of Estonia is coming next week. He especially asked to meet you at the state dinner we're giving for him."

"I'll come for coffee."

"People will notice that you didn't eat the entire dinner."

"I am only human, and I can do just so much."

"What is more important than Estonia?"

"Staten Island."

"Did you know, Hillary, that at my last press conference they asked me if the country still has a First Lady? I told them that as far as I was concerned that's all you are interested in as long as I am in office."

"My campaign people were very unhappy when you said that. Your answer should have been 'She's my First Lady now, but she will be your First Lady next November.' Good-bye. I have to catch the Metroliner."

"When will you be back?"

"Sometime after the Sons of Naples spaghetti dinner in Syracuse."

Millennium Eve

IF AMERICANS FOLLOW THE SCRIPT, most people will be home on the evening of the millennium rather than carousing in bars and on the streets. They will be watching television, which has gone all out to produce the biggest shows in history to welcome the year 2000.

The problem for the stay-at-homes, as I see it, is who will control the television remote control. The person who holds the clicker in his hand has the power to bring in the New Year all around the world.

It is a responsibility so great that only the best and brightest will be permitted to put their fingers on the channel button.

I predict that this could happen in a typical American household:

Tucker Gibson grabs the clicker before his wife can touch it. He tells her, "Tonight is too important to let an amateur surf."

This doesn't go over very well with Edith. "Tucker," she says, "you had the remote for the entire decade. I want to bring in the year 2000."

"It's too risky. I am the only one in the family who knows how to select a channel with my eyes shut."

"Change to ABC. I understand Peter Jennings is on for twenty-four hours."

"If that is true, we can always get to ABC later. Let us see what NBC is doing."

Young Reg Gibson says, "Switch to MTV. I'm sure they have a better show."

Gibson replies, "Do you mind if I do the clicking?"

Edith complains, "You just went by CNN. I think we should at least see what the people in Baghdad are doing."

Gibson says, "If we watch CNN then we also have to watch Geraldo Rivera on MSNBC."

Young Reg says, "What station is carrying *Who Wants to Be a Millionaire?*"

"They're not showing it on New Year's Eve."

"Why not?"

"For the same reason they're not showing Guy Lombardo. Everyone be quiet. I'm going to surf to Mike Wallace."

"Why Wallace?"

"He'll tell us who the crooks will be in the New Year."

Edith asks, "Couldn't I click once for good luck?"

Gibson answers, "You can if you promise to give it right back to me."

Edith takes the remote, and the screen goes blank.

"What happened?"

Young Reg says, "I think it's the Y2K bug."

"Give it to me," Gibson demands. "It's almost midnight."

Reg does the countdown. "Ten, nine, eight, seven, six, five, four, three, two, one."

Gibson yells, "Bingo!" and pushes the remote button. On the screen he gets the wrestling channel—the only one that is working.

And that is how the Gibsons and many others will bring in the first day of the next two thousand years.

Millionaire Fever

I ATTENDED A DOT.COM CONVENTION the other day. A dot.com convention is where all the geniuses on the Internet and in the computer profession meet to divvy up what's left of the Web sites in the world as well as Bulgaria.

It took me a few days to get the hang of the convention. I discovered the guys with holes in their black sweaters without undershirts were billionaires.

Those who wore shirts, ties and jackets were still trying to sell their companies to anybody. And the ones of that bunch on cell phones were trying to explain to their landlords why they couldn't pay their rent until July.

A third group at the convention was the venture capitalists, who had money to burn on any new technology—even from Bulgaria.

There was a Pac-Man atmosphere at the convention. The venture capitalists were chasing the nerds, the people wearing jackets and shirts were chasing the venture capitalists, and the billionaires were playing Ping-Pong in Bill Gates's Microsoft hospitality suite.

Everyone was hoping to come up with a faster way to send e-mail through a broadband or via a computer that plays Beethoven's Ninth Symphony while an airline puts you on hold.

I met one venture capitalist who said he had $100,000,000 to invest in any new system as long as it could order James Joyce and sing the national anthem of Bulgaria.

Everyone was nice to everyone. The Yahoo network was giving away free frankfurters in its suite, which attracted almost all the telephone executives.

There was some question raised as to whether royalties should be paid to writers for their property.

"That would be foolish," a hardware manufacturer said. "If we start compensating writers, it will set a precedent."

Someone from the audience asked, "Then how do you compensate writers for their work?"

A dot.com entrepreneur said, "Through goodwill."

By accident I was wearing a black moth-eaten sweater one day and was mistaken for a billionaire.

A venture capitalist was immediately on my trail. He said, "Before you sell your interactive video game, talk to us. We have money to burn."

I realized I was being taken for a very rich nerd.

"I am not for sale and neither is Dungeons & Slimy Mud," I told him.

The venture capitalist said, "For Heaven's sake, man, don't you want to go public?"

"But you don't even know me," I said.

"You haven't shaved for three days, and that's good enough for me."

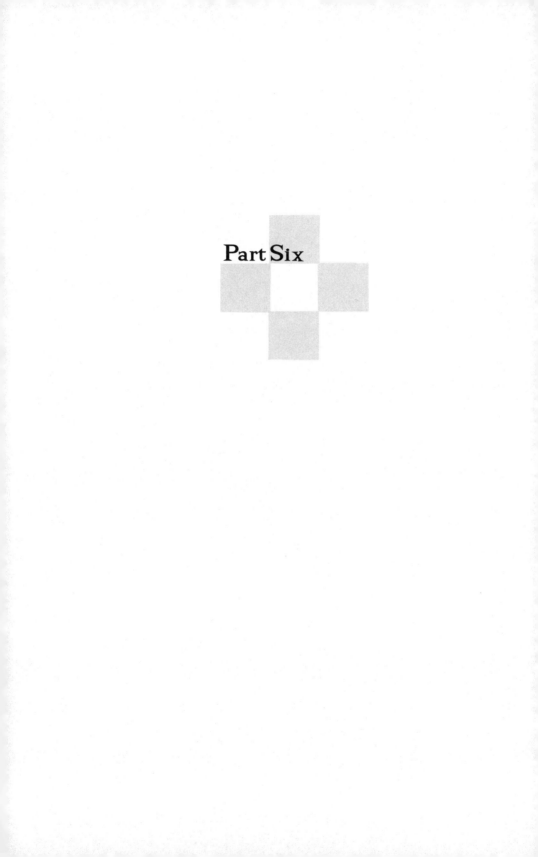

Part Six

Back to Work

THIS IS WHAT I DID on my vacation. I had a stroke. It tied me up for three months, two of which I don't remember. I won't bother you with the details, because I'm not aware of them myself. I was in a world of my own, even more secret than the FBI Witness Protection Program. What I did find when I woke up was a support scene of doctors and nurses from Georgetown University Hospital and the National Rehabilitation Hospital who spent hours, weeks and months to get me better.

When you go through something like this, people expect you to come out looking like Howard Hughes. Doctor Michael Newman; my three children Joel, Connie and Jennifer; and countless strangers decided instead that I should look like Jimmy Stewart in *It's a Wonderful Life*.

Once you get into a hospital situation, you realize how dedicated people in the health field are. Medicare, Medicaid, HMOs
and all such programs are the business of politicians and businessmen. Taking care of people is the role of the doctors, nurses
and technicians whose first job is to get you healthy.

I wish I could tell you what it was like, but I don't remember.
My doctors and children said I behaved badly. My son, in discussing this, said, "You should have been there, Dad."

A stroke strikes unexpectedly. It plays havoc with the cells in
your brain. Medical teams and counselors have to help you put all
the cells back together again.

This took all sorts of exercises by people whose sole job was
to undo the damage. The work done at the National Rehabilitation Hospital could be compared to medical boot camp. You are
assigned exercises to facilitate walking again and getting your
memory back. I learned how to get into the seat of a car again,
move my legs and climb stairs. In many cases the mind forgets,
and you have to deal with relearning everything, from names of
people you know to the history of your own life.

I'm getting this out of my system, and I won't deal with it again.
If there is anything that really stays with me, it's that I have to
maintain a diet of two thousand calories a day.

I think more about this than any other part of the illness. Food
has always been good to me, and I have always been good to food.
At one time a chocolate éclair was the Viagra in my life. Now eating an extra handful of grits is a venal sin. I go to restaurants and
watch with awe as people cut into their juicy steaks and French
fries, and I ask why them and not me.

I am not complaining about a diet, but the closer it comes to dinnertime the closer I get to wanting to eat the pizza off the television screen.

I won't bother you anymore with this. Hundreds of friends and strangers wrote me letters when I was sick. I thank them one and all—even though many of them offered to buy me a luscious dinner when I got well.

Craps

THE TRUTH IS THAT EVEN FOR RICH PEOPLE there are good days and bad days on the stock market. The other day was a bad day, and billionaires lost a bundle. How do rich people deal with bad days? This is my guess.

Bill Gates comes home from the office, and his wife senses something is wrong. "What happened?" she asks while putting his Microsoft slippers on.

"I lost twelve-point-one billion dollars today."

Mrs. Gates says, "That's terrible. Does this mean I can't cover the couch in the living room?"

"No, you can't. I'm not made of money."

"If you keep losing in the stock market, I am never going to get the living room done."

Bill Gates says, "If we do the couch, I'll only have seventy-one billion left."

Mrs. Gates replies, "It doesn't hurt to spend a few bucks to make the house look pretty."

Just then the phone rings. Gates says to his wife, "It's Steve Ballmer. He lost three-point-seven billion in Hong Kong."

Mrs. Gates says, "What's the big deal? Tell him all of us lose some and win some—as long as we don't lose our private planes."

Bill Gates says, "Steve wants to know if he can borrow a couple of billion so he can fix his driveway."

Just then the doorbell rings. It's Charles Ergen of EchoStar, who has lost a million. He has a racehorse tied to him. He says to Gates, "Would you like to buy the next Kentucky Derby winner?"

Gates says, "I'm tapped out. I can't even afford a paralegal to fight my antitrust case."

There is disappointment on Ergen's face. "It was your case that made the market do a nosedive. The least you can do is buy my horse."

The next one to show up is Henry T. Nicholas III, of Broadcom. He says to Gates, "I know it isn't many big bucks to you, but I lost nine hundred thirty-nine million dollars yesterday."

"Not to worry," Bill says. "I'm not in great shape either. I wanted to refurbish my yacht, but I'm going to postpone it until the market goes up."

Henry says, "It's not me. It's my wife. She's afraid that she is going to have a bad hair day."

Gates says, "Henry, the only thing you can do is cut back on your more expensive wines and skip the truffles on your salad. Look, we're in a business where one day you're up and the next day you're in the sewer. That's what being a billionaire is all about."

"Suppose I lose a billion in the market? Will that hurt my credit?"

"It doesn't matter as long you get respect on the Internet."

Tickets, Please

WE HAVE DOZENS OF ORGANIZATIONS involved with air safety. The only place where we seem to be weak is selling an airline ticket at the airport. While great strides have been made in everything from communications to questionable food, a big glitch in the airline business takes place when you go up to the airline counter to check in.

The tough part of purchasing a ticket is watching the airline clerk in slow motion wrestling with his (or her) computer. All information concerning your trip to Santa Fe has to be sent to Nome, Alaska. No one is skillful enough to feed this vital material correctly the first time around, so the agent has to keep repeating it until she (or he) gets it right.

The average time for entering information into a computer, not counting a lunch break, is twenty-five minutes. It is much longer if you are going to change planes in Atlanta.

But where it really gets screwed up is if you have a nighttime fare that you are trying to use in the daytime—or a daytime fair you are using at night, or a frequent-flyer fare that cannot be used if you are going through Cincinnati.

The computer is attached to a black box, which the agent turns on when he wants to inspect your driver's license. This causes some problems when the plane you are scheduled to fly on has already closed its gate.

Now what makes flying such a gamble is that most airline computers are outdated, and they crash just as you get to the counter.

Once the airline agent gets everything ready to go, he then has to use his staple machine to staple the ticket to the baggage claim. Unlike gun registration, all staple machine operators have to be registered, and their records are sent to Washington.

Every piece of paper on the airline counter has to be stapled twice and then stapled again, whether the flight is confirmed or not. Because of the heavy load, the airlines run out of staples before they run out of tickets. Some flights have been delayed until a new supply of staples arrives.

I am an expert at waiting at airline counters. It is the most interesting part of flying. Where it gets really exciting is when they don't find your name in the computer. Airline clerks enjoy this because the search is on. What makes it dangerous is that the people behind you want to kill you. The biggest honor you can receive is to have your clerk call his supervisor. Now there are two airline employees on your case.

I can't complain that airline counter people are not nice to me. Most of them enjoy what they are doing and are delighted when my reservation has fallen out of their machine.

One time I got past the computer, and I thought I was home free. I felt really good about it until they wouldn't let me on the plane.

Ninety Miles Away

THIS COUNTRY IS DIVIDED over the Elian Gonzalez case. Did Attorney General Janet Reno do the right thing? Was Elian's father entitled to custody of his child, and should the Miami relatives keep suing whomever it is they're supposed to sue?

The one person who seems to be having a ball is Fidel Castro. For several years Castro has been a forgotten man in the United States, except by tourists who have been anxious to buy illegal cigars there. Long ago Castro was mentioned by old-timers as that man who lived ninety miles away from Miami, Florida. The Cubans in Florida were the only ones who mentioned Castro's name, but not in a very friendly way.

It has been no fun for Castro to be ignored all these years. Since the Cuban Missile Crisis in the '60s, which almost started World War III, Castro has become a minor figure in major world decisions. His warnings to the United States went unheeded, and his beard became scragglier as the years went by. It was a rare evening when he appeared on the evening news, and no one tuned into CNN just to hear him.

Then Elian came on the scene, and Castro suddenly had a cause to rev up his people. This included six-hour speeches at the airport and all over the rest of Cuba.

So it turned out that Castro was becoming a big-time leader. He started telling President Clinton what he wanted done. Every news show, as well as CNN, now has reporters in Havana.

The Cuban-Americans in Miami were as mad at Castro as ever. There were suggestions from Little Havana to organize and attempt another Bay of Pigs since it didn't work the first time. Janet Reno turned the idea down. Then someone talked about poisoning Castro's cigar, which we had tried once before without success.

No matter what happens, Castro is back, and we have to deal with him.

I have no suggestion except to trim his beard.

I guess the thing that hurts Americans and Cuban-Americans is that Elian will be returning to Havana. If we had our choice, he would remain in the United States. It would be a happy ending to the story, and it would make Castro look bad.

But we can't do anything to stop him or keep the refugee boats from coming across the sea.

Personally, every so often I wish that Castro would stop being ninety miles away.

Happy Graduation

I ATTENDED MY FIRST college graduation this year. It was different from previous ones. I discovered that this is the first class that is more interested in investing money than they are in the opposite sex.

As the students filed down the aisle, I noted that half of them were talking into cellular phones. I asked a young man wearing a cap and gown whom he was calling. He said, "My broker, Charles

Schwab. He told me to call him this morning in case he had some good news for me. He said with all the kids playing the market I have to keep my eye on the ball."

"I didn't know your class was so involved in the stock market."

"Big time. You see that guy in front of me? He made thirty-five thousand dollars in Yahoo shares while failing civil engineering."

"That's impressive."

"It's nothing compared to the guy sitting over there drinking beer. He invested in Amazon and lost all his tuition money, so they wouldn't let him graduate."

"How did this generation manage to invest so big?"

"We all have computers. If we couldn't afford one, the school would lend us one. The university would rather that students play Wall Street than have frat parties when the market closes down."

Standing in front of the young man was a lady in cap and gown. She had tears in her eyes. "I hate to lose money on Time Warner on the day of my graduation. My daddy said I'm never going find a husband if I keep dating bears."

The person behind her said, "Can I borrow your laptop? I just heard that Greenspan will lower the interest rates before we get our diplomas."

The most interesting thing that happened was when the students took their seats, they all opened the *Wall Street Journal.*

The graduation speaker tried to instill some noble thoughts, but the students weren't buying any. Instead they were sending buy-and-sell signals to each other. The only time the students paid attention was when the speaker attacked the unfairness of the government suit against Microsoft. "Bill Gates showed us the way. If there is any injustice in the world it's when people try to break up Windows 98."

A young man said, "I wish he would talk more about soybeans and less about our futures."

After the graduation I wandered over to the campus. I heard a father say to his son, "If you put your money in British Airways, then you'd better find a job." A mother said, "Don't come back home with a recession."

The president of the school was not too disturbed with the graduates' interest in the stock market. "If these kids make it big in the Nasdaq, we'll assign each of them a gifts advisor and I'll get my library built before Walt Disney takes a bath."

"Do you admire this generation more than the last?"

"It depends on what they're holding in their portfolios."

Harry Pinkney Day

IT HAD TO HAPPEN sooner or later. Marcy Department Store had run out of holidays to celebrate.

The top guns called in Harry Pinkney, from the notions department, and said, "Harry, we have celebrated George Washington's Birthday, Lincoln's Birthday, Valentine's Day, Veteran's Day, Fourth of July, Labor Day, the Marines' Birthday, Thanksgiving, of course, Christmas and New Year's, plus Miracle Day, Pearl Harbor Day and Halloween. The truth is, if you look at the advertisements, we have nothing left to celebrate."

Harry looked bewildered. "I don't see what this has to do with notions."

"We want to celebrate your birthday. Our customers will get fifty percent off on Harry Pinkney's Birthday at Marcy."

"I appreciate it very much, but no one gives a tootler's damn about my birthday. Even my wife doesn't celebrate it anymore."

"That's just the point, Harry. Marcy's cares as much for the little fellow as we do the giants like Christopher Columbus and the store's founders. People will want to know who Harry Pinkney is. You will be famous overnight. We'll put your photo in every display window, and you will appear on television plugging Marcy's sales. We'll make a whole new line of Harry Pinkney silk pajamas and underwear, and whoever wins the Marcy Sweepstakes gets to spend twenty minutes in the notions department with the once most uncelebrated man in America."

"I don't know. I'm not one of those who sticks out in a crowd."

"Now here's your blockbuster. We will make a rubber balloon that will be bigger than anything they fly at Macy's. And you will be driven down Broadway in a super convertible."

"Will I get credit for sales in my notions department for flogging for Marcy?"

"Of course you will. We might even promote you to ladies' cologne."

"I'm going to have to talk this over with my wife."

"Don't stall, Harry. We may go with Sam Huggens in fine handbags."

"Will you celebrate Harry Pinkney Day every year?"

"No, you idiot, just once. After you become a household word, you'll be famous for fifteen minutes. You will have served Marcy, and we will never forget you. We may even allow you to eat in the executives' dining room on your special day. But don't let it go to your head. You're not going to get stock options for your birthday."

"Suppose someone finds out my real birthday is in April?"

"It won't bother them as long as we give them a parade with Regis Philbin down Broadway."

Payback

IT IS PAYBACK TIME for the politicians. The election is finally over, and people are now wanting to collect on their contributions.

Junker, in charge of Junker Pharmaceuticals, showed up at the White House with his wife, carrying a mattress, quilt and sheets.

The guard at the gate asked him what he was doing there.

Junker replied, "Marian and I want to sleep in the Lincoln Bedroom as agreed with Harry Kornblambast of President-Elect Bush's soft-money committee in Louisiana."

"But the new president won't move in until January 20, 2001."

"Harry didn't say anything about this when he accepted my check."

"Why don't you come back?" the guard asked.

"I don't have time. Besides, it isn't easy to drag this mattress and quilt down here."

"What are you going to do with them?"

"We always carry our own bedclothes. Marian never likes to sleep in the White House in somebody else's sheets."

"You'd better come back in January."

"I have to see the president right away. I was told I could talk to him about raising the price of pharmaceuticals as soon as he was elected."

"The only one here is Bill Clinton."

"What is wrong with seeing him?"

"He has no real power to do anything about pharmaceuticals."

"What time is the state dinner tonight?"

"Why do you want to know?"

"Harry told us that for a hundred thousand dollars we could attend a state dinner at the White House."

Marian asked, "Can I use the White House hairdresser?"

The guard said, "I don't know what Harry promised, but nothing for new soft-money givers starts until January twentieth."

Junker said, "Before the election Harry called me every week for a contribution to his soft-money group. Now when the election is over, I can't even get through to him on his e-mail."

"Mister, do you mind getting your bedding out of here? You're attracting the homeless."

"The pharmaceutical industry will think twice when the next election rolls around. Can we at least have a nap in the Rose Garden?"

"Hillary has some friends there now who are taking a snooze. And two more people from Queens who are waiting in line."

Junker seemed embittered. "Don't you people honor your political promises anymore?"

"We do the best we can. The White House police have no control over soft-money donors. That's handled by the secretary of the treasury."

A Great Skier

I AM NOT FOR GIVING presidential pardons willy-nilly, but when a Marc Rich comes along, I say let him go free. Rich made his home in Switzerland because he is an avid skier, collects watches and likes to yodel.

There are lots of stories about how Rich was pardoned by the president. One I heard was that the president, on his last night in office, was signing pardons for his half brother and other worthy supplicants. Suddenly a lawyer came in and said, "Sir, before you sign any other pardons, I've got the perfect candidate. He is the best American skier in Switzerland."

"Why does he need a pardon?"

"I don't know, but the man is a fantastic skier. He has won the Davos Downhill, the Kloster Slalom and the Gstaad Cross Country. The American Olympic team needs him badly, but some pencil pusher in the Justice Department is trying to keep him out of the country."

"What else has he done to rate a pardon?"

"His ex-wife gave a million dollars to your "get well" campaign fund, and she threw in a couple of coffee tables and two swell chairs—but she said it had nothing to do with the pardon. By the way, she's a good skier too."

"How do we know Rich wants to come back to the U.S.?"

"We don't know, but he still should have the choice. As it stands now, every time his helicopter goes up in the air there is always a chance it will land in France and he'll be arrested."

"It makes a lot of sense to pardon someone rich instead of someone poor. Is it true he sells and buys Iraqi oil?"

"I haven't gone into his private life. All I know is he's a very charitable person and gives away a lot of money to political causes."

"I would like to pardon him," Clinton said, "but I'm pardoning a hundred and forty people people tonight, and my hand is getting tired."

"I'll bet not one of the people you're setting free is a great skier. If I can talk him into coming, and I'm not saying I can, I'm sure he would build a ski lift in Chappaqua."

"How is his golf game?" the president asked.

"He won the Geneva Tax Fraud Open last year. We're talking about an all-around athlete."

"Okay, but I'm only doing it because we need American skiers who live in Switzerland."

Layoffs

IN REGARD TO LAYING OFF people at AOL–Time Warner, Mr. Robert W. Pittman, a chief executive, said, "The layoffs represent pain because it is people, and people you like, but you have to align the company with the mission. By moving quickly we can start focusing on building."

Some people at AOL were angry at being pink-slipped. But others felt that even though they were being fired it was good for the merger.

Harvey Blankenship came home to break the news to his wife. "I was blown away by AOL–Time Warner today."

Mrs. Blankenship was angry. "How could they do that to you?"

"We have to think of the company first. It couldn't have duplication of jobs because when you merge there has to be pain. I'm not big on pain, but I have to agree that trimming fat is the first priority. And the big shots can't do their jobs if the little guys are still drawing their paychecks."

Harvey's wife was still angry. "You sound like you went quietly into the night."

"Well, I didn't raise a stink like some of the guys. Errol Fligor called a union meeting to protest the dismissal, which made the executives angry. The last thing you want when they kick you out the window is a strike. Arnie Locust said he was organizing a boycott of AOL. Management pointed me out as someone who understands how much the company needed to lose my job. To show their appreciation for the way I behaved, they let me stay for lunch."

"Harvey, if it didn't mean losing our medical plan, your paid vacations—and your parking place—not to mention your salary I would say you did the right thing."

Harvey replied, "The most important thing a corporation must have to survive is restructuring. If that has a price to it, so be it."

"Will we still see our friends?"

"We won't see those who are still working, but we can play all the golf we want to with those who were laid off."

Harvey's wife said, "Did they say they would help you find another job?"

"Come to think of it, it never came up. They were waiting by the water cooler to pink-slip me, and I could see pain on their faces. I felt it was my duty to accept the pink slip and keep walking toward the door."

Harvey's wife said, "They'll remember you, and when they restructure you'll be the first person they call back."

"Right—and the next time I'll be mean and lean like everybody else."

Clinton Sightings

EVER SINCE THE INAUGURATION, there have been sightings of former president Bill Clinton all over town. One of my sources said that he saw Clinton at the Palm Restaurant with several people he had pardoned on his last day in office. The only thing different about this luncheon is that everyone went Dutch and Clinton ate a hot fudge sundae, which he made everybody promise not to tell Hillary about.

The next sighting was at the Burning Tree Country Club, where Clinton was playing golf with Vernon Jordan. Clinton laughed a lot when he played, had a hot fudge sundae and gave his caddy five dollars.

I thought I had heard the last of Clinton that day when someone called from Georgetown to tell me the ex-president was seen in an anti–school voucher protest parade. Clinton bought a hot fudge sundae in the Häagen-Dazs store on Wisconsin Avenue.

Bill then tried to get into the Senate building to see Hillary, but he was stopped at the door because he carried a sign that was too large. He had the guard call up Hillary, who told her aide to let him in the building.

My source reported that Bill threw himself on Hillary's floor and had to be dragged out by the Capitol police.

My informant reported that Hillary said she would discuss Bill's sit-in with him when she got home that night.

It was quiet in my office until six o'clock, when I had a report that Clinton was seen at a shopping mall. He was eating a Big Mac and a chocolate milk shake while talking to a shopper who recognized him from his days as president. Bill took out a list of his accomplishments, which he always carries with him in case he runs into this situation. The shopper asked if he would address his Kiwanis club, and Bill said he was awfully busy these days but he would think about it.

It was getting dark, and Hillary called on her cell phone to say they were debating an abortion bill and she wouldn't be home for dinner.

Clinton had no choice but to go to a movie. He chose *Traffic*, where he accidentally met the husbands of other Senate wives.

"What do we do now?" one of the husbands asked after the film.

"I'm going to stay up and wait until Hillary comes home."

"What a great life you have," another husband said.

"But we don't have to hurry home. First let's all have a hot fudge sundae."

A Trillion Here, a Trillion There

IT WAS BIG NEWS that the federal budget surplus for the next ten years will come to 5.610 trillion dollars, or nearly one trillion more than expected. This, of course, is good news for all of us, though we still don't know how the bean counters could be off by so much. What kind of accountants do we have in the government who can't even put the decimal point in the right place?

Once the mistake was revealed, the argument was what to do with the money. We barely were going to get by on $4,650,000,000,000, but now that we'll have $5,610,000,000,000, we'll have money to burn.

Already Congress is arguing about it. The Democrats want to pay back some of the debt so we can't enjoy the surplus.

The Republicans want to give it back to us on the grounds that it was our money in the first place.

It has become a bone of contention in Washington, not only with the big shots but also for the man in the street.

Ham Forester, who lives down the street, said, "If you gave me the five trillion, my wife would spend it on shoes. I'd rather we use it to pay for baseball salaries."

Blair St. Ledger-Olson said, "They will promise us a trillion and then use it for elections in Florida. I say let's use the money to pay back the friends of the Clintons."

Martindale said, "Give me a trillion and I'll pay off my mortgage."

I said, "We all keep talking about five trillion dollars, but how do we know it is there?"

St. Ledger-Olson agreed. "I've not seen even one trillion dollars, much less five. They must have it stashed away in a numbered account in Switzerland."

"The president maintains that he's seen the five trillion dollars and that he wants to give it away to jump-start the economy."

"I don't think a lousy five trillion dollars is going to do it. You're still going to have to pay for electricity in California."

"Maybe we should use it for Medicare and Social Security."

"That's a dumb thing to do with it. After all, it is our surplus, and the kids today should pay for their own Medicare and Social Security."

Ham Forester said, "I'm sorry they brought it up in the first place. Everyone knows that what the government promises with one hand it takes away with the other."

Beautiful Dreamer

WHAT PRESIDENT BUSH IS is a beautiful dreamer. He dreams great things for our economy. He dreams that his tax cuts will solve all our problems—and mainly he dreams that if we can invest our Social Security money privately we can do much better than if the government does it for us.

When my broker called, I said, "Those are all good dreams, and

I'm glad he has them. But how do you know that what he dreams is going to happen?"

My broker replied, "All I know is that I have some hot stocks to sell you."

"This is my Social Security. I don't want to waste it."

"How could you lose money in the stock market?"

I replied, "That's a good question."

My broker said, "It's true the stock market has gone down, but if you'd invested your Social Security in 2000 you'd be one rich man."

"This is 2001 and I've taken a bath."

He said to me, "Social Security is like a crap game. You lose one day and gain the next. It's better to roll the dice in the NASDAQ than have the bureaucrats in Washington put your money in stuff that takes the thrill out of your pension plan."

I said, "If I'm going to invest in something, it has to be AT&T."

My broker said, "We have a saying at the firm that AT&T used to be the stock *for* widows and orphans, but now it *makes* widows and orphans."

"Why does the president dream that older people can invest their money so well?" I asked.

"Because he thinks that even with a bear market the public is going to come out ahead. And if they don't, the brokers will. Besides, if we're going to put aside two trillion for our old age, the American people have to believe the president's dream is their dream."

"Has Bush figured out how he wants to do it?"

"No, but fortunately he will appoint a commission to study it. Presidents dream the best when they have a commission to study the dream. The way Mr. Bush figures it out, the baby boomers will be hitting sixty-five, and Wall Street is waiting for them."

I said, "My fear is that the baby boomers will go into a frenzy if the stock market jumps off a cliff. Can you imagine what they will do if they lose their savings?"

He said, "Mr. Bush would never dream of that."

Keeping Down with the Joneses

WHEN THINGS WERE GOOD, the Havenots always tried to keep up with the Joneses. They, of course, couldn't, as the Joneses were the big spenders on the block.

Now it's an entirely different story.

Jerry Havenot told me about it. "The Joneses are acting queer," he said. "I stopped over at their house, and instead of a new Lexus in the driveway there was a 1983 Toyota. He said that he got tired of the Lexus and that the Toyota was much more comfortable because it only had a hundred and twenty-three thousand miles on it.

"Two days later I was invited for dinner at the Joneses' home. There were several empty spots on the wall where Jones used to hang signed Picasso, Chagall and da Vinci prints. Brennon Jones said he was getting tired of the prints and thought the house was more attractive without paintings. Usually the Joneses serve a French dinner consisting of foie gras, Dover sole, rack of lamb, a salad and baked Alaska, complimented by a Château Haut-Brion. This time we had spaghetti with tomato sauce and a rotgut table wine from the wrong part of Italy.

"The table conversation then turned to clothes. Marion Jones said she was no longer going to Christian Dior because everything she wanted she could find at Kmart. Brennan said he stopped buying clothes at Calvin Klein as he could get the same type of clothes at Syms for one-tenth the price.

"This made my wife, Hilda, feel better because she had a problem keeping up with Marion's wardrobe, particularly at country club luncheon functions.

"From there we went on to schools. The Joneses said they were pulling their son out of Princeton and enrolling him at Staten Island Community College, where Brennan said he could get the same education for practically nothing.

"That night when we got home I said to my wife, 'Is it just my imagination, or is there something going on with the Joneses that we don't know about?'

"She said, 'Well, they are easier to keep up with than ever before. They always talked about how great their stocks were doing. Tonight there wasn't a peep out of them.'

"I said, 'Did you notice after dinner she was darning his socks?'

"She replied, 'The tip-off for me was when Brennan said they had decided to stay home this summer and rent out their house on Martha's Vineyard. Has it ever occurred to you that the Joneses may have to live up to us rather than vice versa?'

"I told Marion, 'I never thought I'd see the day when he'd be driving a Toyota and I would be driving a new Pontiac.'

"Marion asked me, 'Is our boy still dating one of the Jones girls?'

"I told her, 'Over my dead body.'"

Mean Television

TELEVISION IS GETTING MEANER AND MEANER. The "survival" shows depend on meanness to hold the audience's interest. And now there is *Weakest Link,* featuring Anne Robinson, an English scold. She has created a hit by telling her contestants to take a walk because they are the weakest link in the chain.

Whereas in the past you were rooting for your man or woman contestant, now your enjoyment comes from seeing either one fall flat on his or her face. Ms. Robinson is in the humiliation business, and the NBC network couldn't be happier.

What is the reason, you ask, for the turnaround?

Fred Archmeddy, a programming vice president, said it is the age factor. "We only want young people from ages thirteen to thirty-nine watching. These are the people who buy our products, and we'll give them any program they want if they will just watch our show."

I said, "Then programming for those over forty is a waste of time."

"You better believe it. The culture is with the young. It happens that young people seem to like mean. They like it in the movies, they like it on television and they like it in life. Anne Robinson is a perfect role model. She is a stern-looking schoolmarm, a Margaret Thatcher if you've ever seen one. When you make a mistake, she takes it out of your hide. The truth is, she's a bitch and that's the way NBC likes her. When she tells panelists 'good-bye' it's really good-bye, except that they have to humiliate themselves one more time after she kicks them off the air. They're taken into a room, and they tell the audience how unfair she was to them."

"*XFL,* the football bomb, was a humiliating show, but despite its meanness it didn't attract a very large audience."

Archmeddy said, "Not every mean show is a smash. The young audience didn't go for it, even though they went for wrestling. But we're not giving up. We'll keep humiliating people no matter how nasty, as long as it produces ratings."

"What's your definition of a successful lousy show that draws crowds?"

"Look at *Survivor* and all the copycat shows in which people are really mean to each other. That's great television as long as it sells Dracula Beer."

"Don't you have any shows for audiences over thirty-nine?"

"It's a waste of time. Anyone over thirty-nine, as far as TV is concerned, is over the hill. All people over thirty-nine do is write letters complaining that our shows are too mean. The networks refer to these people as 'demographically unfit.'"

The Good Guys

I AM SICK AND TIRED of everyone picking on the airlines. It's about time someone said nice things about them, such as:

1. Where can you get a tastier and more nourishing bag of pretzels than on an airplane? The airlines pride themselves

not only on serving pretzels at your seat but also on giving you the choice of peanuts or, in the case of United Airlines, macadamia nuts.

2. More and more airlines are merging, so we don't have to be confused by competition. Depending on the time of day you wish to fly, you can shop around for airfares. For example, at six o'clock in the morning, a fare from Boston to Washington is $300. At lunch it is $600, and at sunset it's $786.56. If you want to change your flight after you purchase a ticket it only costs an extra $100, which can be conveniently charged on your credit card.

3. Concerning luggage, everybody makes a big deal of it when the airline loses their luggage. Only 10 percent of a traveler's luggage gets lost in transit and can usually be found within a week.

4. Most airports have comfortable benches to sit on when your flight is canceled. Also, they all have snack bars where you can have a cup of coffee while figuring out how to get out that day. Also, as the wait increases, you can browse souvenir shops, newspaper stands and even Indian jewelry booths to kill time.

5. All airlines have computers and operators who will check you in. The agents have been sent to a special school and can issue a ticket in thirty minutes unless you're going to Dallas and changing planes for Las Vegas, in which case the computer operator can do it in fifty-five minutes.

6. Airlines get blamed for weather that isn't their fault. For example, going to Atlanta from La Guardia your plane has to first come in from Missoula, Montana. While your weather in New York is good and it's sunny in Atlanta, it's

snowing in Missoula, so you're stuck until the plane arrives. Passengers don't understand weather. *Canceled* is not a dirty word. Airlines use it all the time.

7. Airline rage is becoming a more popular spectator sport. Yelling at an agent is a great way of getting your anger out. If you yell the loudest, you will get the attention of everyone, including the supervisors.

8. Sometimes you will be bumped from a flight because it is overbooked. You should take it in stride and even make a joke out of it. A funny thing to say when being bumped is "Why me?"

9. The nicest thing about flying is how many new friends you can make at airports when your plane is either delayed or canceled. These friendships can last a lifetime.

10. Remember this—airlines are your dearest friends, and you have to understand them. Even after you eat their food.

Bye-Bye, Jeffords

THINGS HAPPEN IN WASHINGTON that do not happen anywhere else. A beauty of an example occurred when Senator James Jeffords left the Republican Party and became an Independent. Ordinarily this wouldn't mean much, because Vermont doesn't mean that much in Washington. But this act of bravery, or treachery, changed the entire voting picture in the capital. It was one small step for Independents and one large step for mankind.

Because he has left his party, all the committee chairmen will have to be changed, and the president will have a much tougher time getting his bills passed.

The talk in Washington is about who was responsible for Jeffords changing his colors.

The guys in the White House refused to take the blame. One said, "I never cared much for the skiing in Vermont."

Another said, "I never liked their maple syrup."

The president said, "That is no reason to kick Jeffords out of the party."

An aide complained, "He was always looking for money for the cattle in Vermont. Every time he came to the White House to get funding for it, we told him to stuff it."

Another one said, "He has such a thin skin. We didn't invite him to the Rose Garden when a Vermont teacher was given a medal, and he thought we weren't treating him with respect. How did we know he was going to walk out on the party? If we knew he was going to make such a fuss over it, we would have given him what he wanted for his educational funds."

The president got madder and madder. "We should have thrown something in for the moderate Republicans."

"If we did, it would have turned the conservative Republicans against us, and we can't afford that."

"I had a long talk with Jim, and he said he was angry because he found out Cheney wants to drill for oil in Vermont."

"Why didn't Cheney tell him there was oil in Vermont?"

"Because before Jeffords walked out no one was taking him seriously. He claimed he had no friends on the Hill, and lobbyists never went to see him."

"So we played hardball," another aide added.

The president sighed. "I was doing so well this week. I got to speak at Yale, my tax bill got through the Senate and I wiped up the oil and energy problems. Now I get blindsided by this."

"Well," said a political advisor, "nobody's perfect."

Greenhouse Gases

AN AIDE WENT INTO the president's office and said, "Mr. President, the office seems very hot."

"Then turn up the air-conditioning. What is it now?"

"It's seventy degrees. I'll turn it down to sixty-five. I wouldn't be able to do this if we had signed the Kyoto treaty, but it's warm outside."

"The people should live where I do in Crawford, Texas. Then they'd know what warm is."

"Here is a report from a distinguished group of scientists who say that global warming is serious."

"Why don't we give them an extra tax cut?"

"Europe is mad at us for not signing the treaty."

"They get mad at everything I do. I'm telling them the only reason I may sign the Kyoto treaty is if they let the U.S. build a missile shield."

"Good thinking, Mr. President. The trade-off is greenhouse gases for a nuclear shield."

"Maybe you'd better put the air-conditioning down to sixty."

"You are the president. You can set it to any temperature you want to."

"China got a waiver, and they are the second-largest emitter of gases. Everyone knows this."

"Who is the largest?"

"We are. And do you know why? We can't get a waiver on the warming. This is what we call a greenhouse effect. When the earth gets warmer, you have no choice but to use more air-conditioning. But using more air-conditioning produces gases. That's why I'm against the Kyoto treaty. I'm as against warming up the earth as the next person, but all in due time. The office is getting warmer."

"We may be having a blackout. The air-conditioning has been cut off."

"Call Kyoto and tell them what's going on."

"There, it's on again."

"I'm setting up a National Climate Change Technology Initiative to measure greenhouse gases. When the temperature rises over a hundred we'll blame it on the Democrats."

"I wish we had taped this conversation."

"The market economy should solve the problem. I am the only one who has said the Kyoto emperor has no clothes on."

"Exactly. Didn't your father reject the Kyoto treaty in Rio de Janeiro nine years ago, Mr. President?"

"He did, and the American people never gave him full credit for it."

"Then you should say when it comes to the greenhouse effect, we'll go it alone. We're at sixty degrees now. Do you want the air-conditioning down to fifty-five?"

"Okay, but give me my coat."

Katharine Graham

KATHARINE GRAHAM CAME INTO OUR LIVES via the *Washington Post* in 1963 when she took over the paper after her husband died. We were quite nervous about the role she would play, and she, in her book, admitted that she was quite nervous, too.

The male journalists were cynical about a woman running "their paper." Her role before this was society woman, hostess and, as she said later on, being a "wife doormat."

But behind her shyness was an extremely sharp mind, and she decided if she was going to be publisher she would have to win over the skeptics. She became close to a small coterie of reporters and editors whom she felt she could trust. She got rid of several who had taken Phil Graham's side when, in a manic state, he took off with another woman.

Her mentor was Ben Bradlee, whom she made managing editor of the paper. Katharine and Ben were a perfect match. They gave each other nourishment. In the beginning Bradlee was the teacher and Katharine was the student. Later on, they became equals—Bradlee the gutsy editor and Katharine the gutsy publisher. Bradlee decided what was news, but she had the final word on what went into her paper.

Her two biggest journalistic triumphs were the Pentagon Papers and Watergate. When the going got rough, she stood by her people.

Katharine was called the most powerful woman in America. She gave lavish dinners for presidents, senators and other people running our country. No one refused her invitations.

While she was entertaining these people, the *Washington Post* was bashing them. I heard her say at dinner when someone complained about a story, "I don't know what I am going to do with Ben Bradlee."

Katharine Graham had a mischievous streak in her. Ben Bradlee, Edward Bennett Williams (the great criminal lawyer) and I used to meet for lunch. We decided to name ourselves "The Club." When Katharine heard about it, she said she wanted to join. We invited her for lunch but said we wanted to make sure she would fit in. We also told her she was the first woman ever to be nominated.

After the lunch Bradlee called her and said, "Kay, I voted for you, but Artie and Eddie were against you." The next call was from me, and I told her, "I don't know how to break this to you. I fought and fought but Ben and Eddie said no way." Eddie made the final call and explained, "I wanted you in the worst way, but Buchwald and Bradlee blackballed you."

She couldn't stop laughing.

Some of her happiest days were spent on Martha's Vineyard. She took her sustenance for the rest of the year from the island. She wasn't Mrs. Graham up there, but "Kay." She was very much involved in Vineyard life. She played a role in conservation. Another thing she did was put herself up every year for an island auction. The winning bidder would have a "Power Lunch" in Washington with Katharine Graham at the *Post*. It was a very hot item, and as the auctioneer, in order to bid it up, I told the audience that if they won it they would be lunching with the most powerful woman in America. Then I added that if she really liked you she would tell you who "Deep Throat" was. It was a lie. But I sold the same lie every year, and it was worth a fortune to the Martha's Vineyard Community Services.

Somebody like Kay Graham comes along once in a lifetime. I'm glad I knew her.

About the Author

Art Buchwald was born in New York, raised as a foster child in Hollis, ran away and joined the Marines at seventeen, then after the war went to USC on the GI Bill, but never graduated. Instead he went to Paris and got a job at the *Paris Herald Tribune*. He never talks about the Pulitzer Prize he won in 1982 unless someone asks him.